Modern Crewel

Embroidery

15 Fresh Samplers Stitched with Wool

stashBOOKS.

Imprint of C&T Publishing

PUBLISHER: Amy Barrett-Daffin

CREATIVE DIRECTOR: Gailen Runge

ACQUISITIONS EDITOR: Roxane Cerda

MANAGING EDITOR: Liz Aneloski

EDITOR: Kathryn Patterson

TECHNICAL EDITOR: Del Walker

COVER/BOOK DESIGNER: April Mostek

PRODUCTION COORDINATOR: Zinnia Heinzmann

PRODUCTION EDITOR: Alice Mace Nakanishi

ILLUSTRATOR: Valyrie Gillum

PHOTO ASSISTANT: Gabriel Martinez

PHOTOGRAPHY by Estefany Gonzalez of C&T Publishing, Inc., unless otherwise noted; photography by Lauren Herberg of C&T Publishing, Inc., on pages 1, 24, 28, 43, 46, 64, 66, 67, 110, and 111 top

Published by Stash Books, an imprint of C&T Publishing, Inc., P.O. Box 1456, Lafayette, CA 94549

Library of Congress Cataloging-in-Publication Data

Names: Avery, Jo, 1966- author.

Title: Modern crewel embroidery : 15 fresh samplers stitched with wool / Jo Avery.

Description: Lafayette : Stash Books, [2021]

Identifiers: LCCN 2021014741 | ISBN 9781644030578 (trade paperback) | ISBN 9781644030585 (ebook)

Subjects: LCSH: Crewelwork--Patterns. | Wool.

Classification: LCC TT778.C7 A94 2021 | DDC 746.44/6--dc23

LC record available at https://lccn.loc.gov/2021014741

Printed in the USA

10 9 8 7 6 5 4 3 2 1

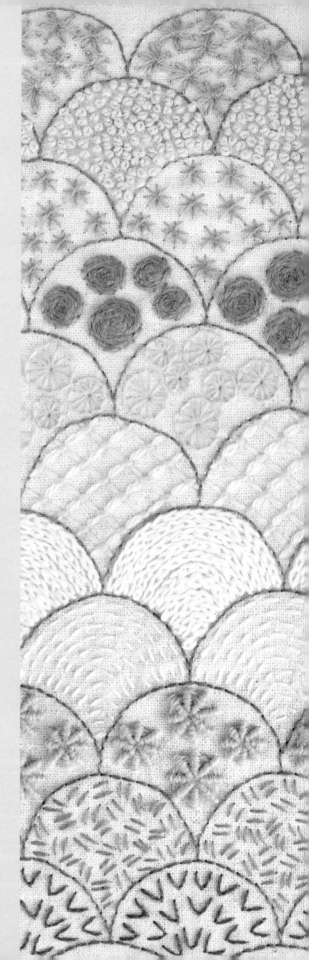

DEDICATION

For my sister, Jane, who taught me to sew

ACKNOWLEDGMENTS

I'd like to thank the following people for enabling me to write this book:

• Aurifil, for your wonderful support and help throughout the last few years. I've loved working with you, hanging out with you all (despite the hangovers!), and look forward to doing the same for many years to come.

• Zweigart for the beautiful linens.

• Auburn Hoops for the stunning hoops.

• Roxane, Liz, Kathy, and all the team at Stash Books for your belief in me, your constant support, and being such a pleasure to work with.

• My best friend, Lisi, for always being there.

• My Thread House Partners and friends Karen and Lynne; I really don't know what I would do without you both. Let's carry on doing this together forever, please.

• My Borders Girls, Patricia, Helen, Donna, Claire, and Ali; your friendship means the world to me.

• My best sewing buddies from around the world: Sarah, Dolores, Pam, Mags, Poppy, Krista, Lorena, Annie, Kerry, Nick, … too many to mention, but I love you all!

• The Super Cubeys, Ali, Tatyana, Sharon, and Kirsten; our karaoke nights keep me sane!

• Helen Addison and Sheila Williams for introducing me to the Spiderweb Stitch and Colonial Knot respectively.

• The Edinburgh Tapestry Tenners; thank you for sharing your skills and friendship.

• My "adopted" daughters Colleen and Katie; so happy you have joined our family.

• My colleagues throughout the years, especially Sarah Roberts, Sarah Vaughan, Barbara, and, of course, Jane.

• And lastly Jonathan, Felix, and Jacob; none of this means anything without you three.

CONTENTS

DOODLES

Doodle Hoop

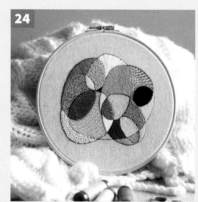

Labyrinth Pouch

NATURE

Scandi Fish Hoop

Arts and Crafts Tree Wallhanging

GEOMETRICS

Honeycomb Hoop

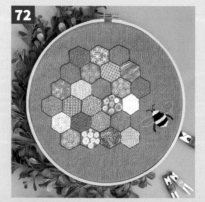

Patchwork Block Mini Hoops

Bubbles Hoop

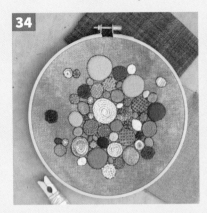

34

Shapes Pincushion Trio

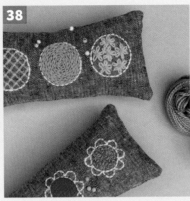

38

Loops Stitch Booklet

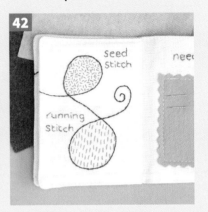

42

seed
stitch

nee

running
stitch

Sea Urchin Pincushion

58

Tendrils Pot

64

Leaf Brooch

68

Cosmic Belt

80

Mandala Hoop

84

Clamshell Pillow

88

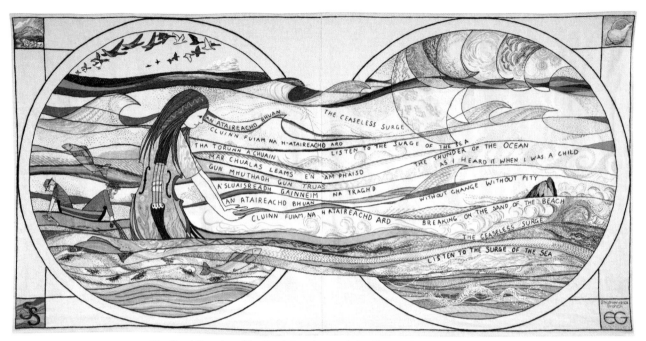

The Great Tapestry of Scotland, Panel 159, stitched by Strathendrick Stitchers

Photo by Alex Hewitt

In progress, detail of The Great Tapestry of Scotland, Welcome Panel, stitched by Welcome Panel Stitchers

Photo by Phil Wilkinson

MY EMBROIDERY JOURNEY

Despite spending much of my childhood sewing and knitting, I only began embroidering seriously a decade ago when I opened my craft studio in Edinburgh, Scotland. I began teaching sewing, quilting, and crochet to a vast army of new recruits, and as there was also a demand for embroidery classes, I added these to the curriculum. I designed a "sampler tree" pattern that enabled me to teach basic stitches, and my skills improved along with those of my students.

In 2013, I heard about a new project to create "The Great Tapestry of Scotland," a vast embroidery that would tell the story of our nation. I immediately volunteered and became part of a local group—the Edinburgh Tapestry Tenners—specially founded for the project. Together we began stitching one of the 165 panels, each depicting and celebrating an episode in Scotland's history, from the last ice age to the twenty-first century. My group included a mix of stitchers from master embroiderers with decades of experience to complete novices, and we all helped and mentored each other during the year it took to finish the panel. This was my real apprenticeship in embroidery—or more accurately, crewelwork. *Crewelwork* simply means embroidery using wool and is the correct terminology for this and other great stitched narratives, such as The Bayeaux Tapestry. Our panel was number five in the story of Scotland, depicting "The Wildwood and Its Fauna c8500BC" (see Panel 5, at right). We were given Appletons crewel wool to stitch the animals and cave dwellers. I fell in love with the soft texture of wool and wanted to use it for more embroidery once the Tapestry project was complete.

But crewel wool can be difficult to obtain with few brands available, and 100% wool thread can be tricky to work with, twisting and breaking easily.

The Great Tapestry of Scotland, Panel 1, stitched by Linda McClarkin and Carol Whiteford

Photo by Alex Hewitt

The Great Tapestry of Scotland, Panel 5, stitched by the Edinburgh Tapestry Tenners

Photo by Alex Hewitt

In 2017, I became an Aurifil Designer and began curating collections from their wide range of beautiful Italian threads. I had been using Aurifil 50-weight thread for patchwork and quilting for many years and was now keen to explore some of their other thread weights for embroidery. I began by using their 12-weight cotton thread which led to a new thread collection inspired by my Passion-flower embroidery design. I loved the bright sheen of the cotton but still longed for the dense matte texture of wool. I decided to experiment with Aurifil 12-weight wool and soon discovered that the effect of crewel wool could be achieved by using two strands together, but with the added advantage of finer detail when using a single strand. As Aurifil wool thread contains around 50% acrylic it has extra strength and doesn't break easily (I even use it in my sewing machine with great success). I began work on my Pebbles Sampler immediately and both a new obsession with modern crewelwork and my next Aurifil collection of the same name began. It was the obvious next step to write and design a whole book of modern crewel embroideries.

Pebbles Sampler,
the initial inspiration
for this book

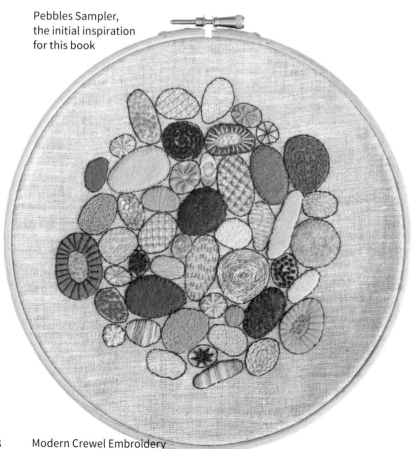

CREWEL EMBROIDERY

The word crewel is an old English or Welsh word meaning wool, which was the traditional material for embroidery. Beginning in the Jacobean era (1603–1625), crewelwork was popular throughout the seventeenth century with traditional crewelwork often referred to by that name. Twisted two-ply wool thread was used to decorate clothing and home furnishings with many of the same stitches still being used today to recreate the look. Traditional crewelwork stitches take advantage of the thickness of wool to create a raised, dimensional feel to the work. In the following collection of sampler embroideries, I have tried to exploit this added texture while offering a new modern twist, simplifying the stitches and aesthetic. Wool is a great choice for embroidery because it works up quickly and the fluffy threads hide imperfections more readily than cotton or silk.

You need little in the way of equipment or material to embark on your first embroidery. As well as accessibility, this means much less impact on the environment than other crafts, such as quilting, especially when wool and linen are chosen over cotton. I have made a conscious effort to use as much natural product as possible in this book. Even though I hope my embroideries will become treasured heirlooms, I am also comforted to know that they will biodegrade easily at some future stage without harming our planet.

Embroidery is not the most forgiving of crafts as your stitching is on display, not hidden as in other sewing. When I first began embroidering, I was in too much of a hurry to finish, my stitching was a little slapdash, and therefore I was not satisfied with the results. I had to learn to slow down and become neater with my stitches. I had to be prepared to take some stitches out if they were not even and try again. Embroidery rewards patience and dedication, and the key is to embrace the slowness rather than begrudge it and enjoy the process as much as the end result. This slow meditative stitching has huge benefits for your mental health, providing the perfect activity to practice mindfulness. You will find yourself calmed and relaxed by the repetitive action of coloring-in with stitches and threads.

HOW TO USE THIS BOOK

The wide range of projects in this book makes it suitable for new embroiderers while hopefully appealing to those who have been stitching for years. If you are a beginner, then start with the simpler projects, such as the Shapes Pincushion Trio (page 38) or the Scandi Fish Hoop (page 48). Achieving a fast finish will be a good motivation for starting another. All the patterns in this book are samplers, traditionally designed to show off a range of stitches and the skills of the embroiderer. Each sampler is made up of similar shapes, which are each filled with different stitches. The fifteen designs can then be turned into a range of imaginative small projects or framed as pictures if you prefer. The basic stitches are explained at the start, with bonus stitches appearing among the projects. I hope this means you will feel less intimidated to begin and can keep adding to your knowledge and skills as you progress through the book.

I have also used felt appliqué to fill some of the shapes on three of the projects. If you like this approach, you can add felt to more of the designs. Once you get the hang of the stitches, I would encourage you to create your own versions, filling areas with whichever stitch you like and not following my instructions too rigorously. Each of the stitches is referred to by the same identifying number throughout, and you will soon learn that a "2" means satin stitch and so on, which will help you decipher the stitch guides. The colors are listed by letter and these change with each pattern. Some stitches, such as laid work, usually include two contrasting colors, and these are indicated on the guides by a slash as in "D/F." The first letter will always be the prominent color with the second being the smaller detail. Of course, you are most welcome to use whichever thread or color you like, wherever you like!

MATERIALS AND EQUIPMENT

FABRICS

You can embroider onto any sort of fabric you like, though textiles with a looser weave tend to be easier to work with. As I come from a quilting background, I like to use the same linen/cotton mix fabrics that I can also utilize for patchwork instead of buying specially made embroidery linens. Most of the projects in this book use Essex Linen by Robert Kaufman, which has a firm stable feel while retaining softness and pliability and is available in a wide variety of shades and finishes. Specialist embroidery linens tend to be stiffer and more unyielding, and I have therefore used these for those projects that would benefit from extra stability, such as the Tendrils Pot (page 64) and the Arts and Crafts Tree Wallhanging (page 52). This type of linen is more prone to fraying, however, so you may want to prepare your edges prior to stitching by using masking tape or stitching a zigzag edge on your sewing machine. For the designs that will end up as pictures in hoops, you can chance lighter fabrics, such as the hand-dyed cotton I used for the Mandala Hoop (page 84) and Bubbles Hoop (page 34), as they will stay permanently stabilized. There is a wide variety of stabilizer materials available that can help with lighter fabric, but I prefer to stitch without and simply match the fabric with the project by suitability.

THREAD

As discussed in the introduction, it was my experiments with Aurifil 12-weight wool thread that led to this book, and I have therefore used this for most of the projects that follow. One of the things I love about the Aurifil wool thread is that it comes on spools rather than skeins and is much easier to handle. As a naturally untidy person, I have always found embroidery skeins very frustrating to use and store. Most of the stitches are worked with two strands of Aurifil wool thread. I start by cutting one long piece that is double the length of a usual strand, and then I thread one end though the needle before knotting the two ends together. This works perfectly for me and the strands rarely separate or twist. The usual advice when cutting a single strand of thread is to knot the end you cut from the spool, which ensures a smoother thread. However, the way I double my thread means that it will run in both directions. Having also experimented with two strands parallel and threaded together through the needle, I can confirm that with wool thread it makes no difference that I can discern.

There are three other threads specified in this book. Appletons crewel wool has a thicker, fluffier texture, which means faster coverage than the Aurifil thread. Vintage Swedish linen threads are thicker still and have a high sheen. Lastly, Aurifil 80-weight cotton is a fine cotton thread used for the felt appliqué. All the designs can be stitched with regular stranded cotton floss or perle cotton and will look equally beautiful, so if you prefer to use your current stock of embroidery threads, please go ahead with my blessing. To help you use other threads, I have compiled a conversion chart from Aurifil wool to DMC cotton, which is on my website (see Resources, page 109).

NEEDLES

Crewel needles are designed for embroidery floss, being of medium length with a sharp point and a long eye to accommodate several thicknesses of thread. These are perfect for the thicker Appletons crewel wool and linen threads. But I prefer to use sharps needles in a size 4 or 5 eye for the finer Aurifil wool thread. They have a smaller round eye and can also be used for any general hand sewing in the book. Choose a good brand of needle, such as Milward, John James, or Tulip.

HOOPS

My preferred hoop is wooden and made by Elbesee. These have a slot in the end of their tightening screw, designed to take a slotted screwdriver, and this enables you to tighten your hoop in a way you couldn't achieve with just the power of your grip. I have suggested a size of hoop for each project, but the choice is a personal one. I find if I choose too large a hoop, it can be difficult to reach the center of the design, making it awkward for some stitches, such as knots. If I choose a smaller hoop, the design might not fit completely, meaning the inconvenience of moving the hoop halfway through stitching. For a special project, I often use a fancier hoop for permanent framing, such as the gorgeous range by Auburn Hoops.

MARKING PENS

Most of the designs need to be traced onto the linen, using lines that you may want to remove later in case anything is still seen after the embroidery is finished. My preferred tool is a Pilot FriXion pen where the marks become invisible with heat from an iron. However, the marks don't go away and can reappear if your embroidery becomes very cold, such as in the hold of an aircraft (something to consider if you are gifting your embroidery overseas!). It can also leave a "ghost line," though this is less of a problem with embroidery where the marks will be too close to the stitching for this to show. There are many other erasable pens available, some that are removed with water, others by air, and I would encourage you to experiment with different methods. For marking on dark fabric, I recommend a Clover white marking pen, which is designed for Sashiko. Always test your marking pens on a scrap of fabric first.

NOTIONS

Here are a few other useful items that may become indispensable to you as you work through this book.

- *Small sharp pair of scissors*
- *Needle threader*
- *Seam ripper*
- *Tracing wheel*—for marking felt
- *Tailor's awl*—for making buckle holes in the Cosmic Belt project (page 80)
- *Screwdriver*—for tightening hoops
- *Appliqué pins*—tiny pins, perfect for holding felt appliqué pieces in place while stitching
- *Toy stuffing (polyester fiberfill)*—for the pincushion projects
- *Batting*—for finishing hoops and in the Tendrils Pot project (page 64)

TECHNIQUES

TRACING

Tracing from the pattern using a lightbox is the quickest and easiest way to transfer the design onto fabric. These days, lightboxes are relatively cheap and readily available at craft stores. Use masking tape to secure both the design and the fabric on top, making sure the fabric is square, that is, that the grain is aligned horizontally and vertically and well stretched. You can make your own temporary lightbox by taking a small shallow cardboard box with no lid (such as a shoebox) and putting your phone inside with the torch function switched on. Place a piece of glass or acrylic, such as a large square patchwork ruler, on the box and trace your pattern on top of this.

Some patterns are given as half of a mirror image to fit within the book page. For these you will need to first trace the design by turning the pattern over so that it is facedown on the lightbox, and draw over the outlines onto the paper. Then trace the pattern from the book again, faceup, onto a separate sheet before taping the two pieces together, aligning the sides to give a perfect mirror image.

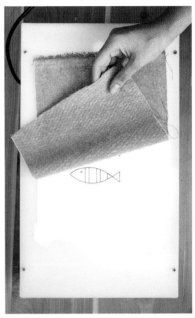

Preparing to trace from pattern to fabric, using a lightbox

Marking Felt

It is almost impossible to see through a dense layer of wool felt, even with a lightbox, so try using a dressmaker's tracing wheel instead. Lay your felt down on top of one or two spare layers of felt and place the paper pattern on top. Trace the lines by pressing down hard on the wheel through the paper. When you take the paper away, there should be enough indentations for you to see the pattern clearly. You can now use your usual marking pen to fill in the lines.

Marking felt using a tracing wheel

HOOPING

Inserting the Fabric

Once you have the design on the fabric, insert it into a suitable embroidery hoop.

Take awhile to position your fabric correctly, pulling and tightening by turn to make sure your fabric is as tight as possible; it should feel like a drum skin. Use a slotted screwdriver to obtain the correct tightness on the fixing screw. If your embroidery is not intended to stay in the hoop, and if you think you may take awhile to finish it, you might like to use a fabric tape to bind the inner ring of your hoop. This prevents marking the fabric and helps hold the fabric securely.

Once it's stitched, you should remove the embroidery from the hoop and press it carefully from the back, using low heat. If you are using wool thread, you need to be extra careful not to scorch the wool. If you need to press from the front as well (to remove stubborn pen marks for instance), I advise placing a pressing cloth, such as a clean tea towel, on top of your embroidery for extra protection.

Finishing a Hoop Back

If your embroidery is going to be framed in the hoop, then re-insert as before. Press the excess fabric to the back and trim away all but ½″ (1cm) from the edge (**fig. A**). Place a piece of scrap fabric, suitable for the lining, underneath and draw around using the outer edge of the hoop. Cut this fabric circle out and press over ¼″ (6mm) seam all the way around the edge (toward the wrong side).

Tip Before stitching the lining in place, I like to put a piece of scrap batting inside the hoop, which I simply cut roughly to size by eye. In some lights, you can see through the linen to the back of the work, and this optional step will help avoid the see-through.

Pin the lining, right side up, to the ½″ (1cm) of the remaining linen. Stitch all the way around using a slip stitch, pulling the two fabrics together firmly with each stitch (**figs. B/C**).

If your hoop isn't a snug fit, you may need to lace your hoop before finishing the back to pull the linen together. Use the strongest thread you can find and take a stitch first at one side of the linen and then the other. Pull the thread tight every few stitches. Repeat to lace the remaining opposite sides together.

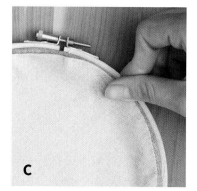

Finishing a hoop back

Tip To give your embroidery frame a special touch, try painting a wooden hoop in a color that matches your embroidery.

STITCH LIBRARY

STARTING AND FINISHING

When working on The Great Tapestry of Scotland, we were warned never to leave knots in the work. Over time and in different temperatures and climates, the threads may move and tighten, and for something that was being stitched for posterity, this was especially important. Therefore, I learned to start stitching using the "waste knot" method and have used this ever since.

Start with a knot on the front of your work, which you will eventually cut off once the thread has been secured by stitches. Make a knot in the end of the thread and insert the needle from the right side, within the area that will be covered by stitching. Work the stitches to fill the area, securing the thread on the back at the same time. Then carefully cut the knot when you reach

it. This can seem a tricky maneuver when you are beginning a piece, especially with your first line of backstitch outline; so keep checking the back and, if necessary, use your needle to weave around the excess thread there and make sure it is caught. Once areas of the design are stitched, you can also weave your starting thread through the stitching at the back, while keeping the knot on the front until it is safe to cut off.

To finish off a thread, simply weave the thread in and out of the stitches at the back of your work before cutting any excess. When using a very stable fabric, such as felt, there is no need to worry about leaving knots long term, so feel free to start with a simple knot at the back and immediately start stitching.

Starting knot

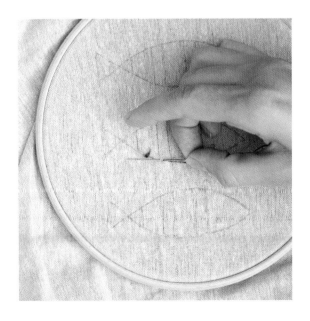

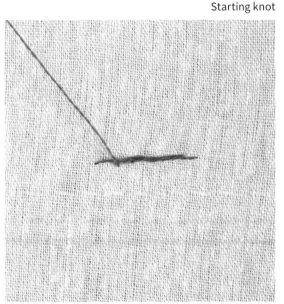

OUTLINE STITCHES

All the projects in this book are outlined with a backstitch. It is my favorite method and gives a clean graphic line.

Backstitch

Working from right to left, bring the needle up through the fabric at A, then back through at B, which will be the actual start of the outline. Bring the needle up again at C, a stitch length in front of A. Repeat the process, going back in again at A, then forward, a stitch length in front at D. Aim to keep each stitch length the same for an even appearance.

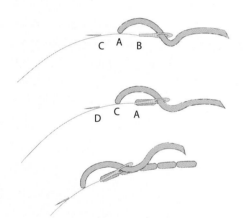

Whipped Backstitch

This extra step gives more emphasis to the outline. Whipping the backstitch will also hide any imperfections and smooth out unevenness of stitches, so feel free to use it even if not instructed in the pattern. It's a very helpful extra step for beginner embroiderers and hides a multitude of sins! Bring the needle up at one end of the line of backstitch and pass the needle under each stitch in turn, always in the same direction, without piercing the fabric.

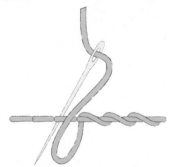

FILLING STITCHES

If you decide not to follow my stitch placings exactly and instead choose to be free and creative with these designs, then it's important to choose the right stitch for the right size of space. For instance, satin stitch cannot be used for a large area as the stitches become too long and may get snagged and pull. Some of the stitches such as the buttonhole wheel are only suitable for larger spaces where they can be used as multiples, whereas the spiderweb stitch can be used as a single stitch to fill a small space or grouped to fill a large space. Starting below are the basic stitches 1–11 you'll be using most frequently; you'll also find the bonus stitches 12–20 (page 23) popping up throughout the projects.

1 Chain Stitch

This is a very versatile filling stitch for all sorts of shapes, with a wonderful texture that almost looks like knitting. Bring the needle up at A, then back down at the same point at B and out again at C, a stitch length along the line, with the tip of the needle over the loop of thread. Pull the thread through to form the first stitch, then take the needle back down through the loop at C and out again at D, a stitch length along the line, with the tip of the needle over the loop of thread once again. Work in close rows to fill the space; these can go up and down or spiraling from the outside in, depending on the size and shape of the area.

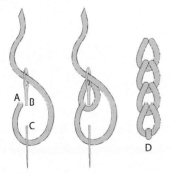

2 Satin Stitch

This classic stitch should lie flat and even and, if worked correctly, give the appearance of satin fabric. I usually find it easier to work from the middle of a shape outward. Bring the needle up through the fabric, just within the outline, and make a long stitch across the shortest side of the shape with the needle going down into the fabric on the other side of the shape just inside the outline. Bring the needle back out right next to the first stitch and make a parallel stitch that lies as close as possible to your first. Continue working out to the edge of the shape before returning to the center and working to the other edge. Satin stitches should be close together and parallel, with no gaps between them, to create a solid area of color. If you find a space between your stitches once you've finished, it's okay to go back and fill it with a single stitch.

3 Colonial Knot

This is my favorite knot and the one I use throughout this book. Most embroidery patterns use French knots; but once you've mastered the colonial, it's hard to go back to a French. A colonial knot looks neater than a French and has a little swirl on the top; plus it also uses less thread. But it does take a little more practice before it feels natural. Bring your thread through to the front of the fabric at A. Hold the thread in your left hand and with your needle pointing away from you and to the left of the thread, slide the needle under the thread, toward the right. Wrap the thread over the needle tip to make a figure eight. Place the needle into the fabric at B, close to where it first emerged but not in the same hole. Before you pull it through, make sure the loop is snug around the shaft of the needle. Pull through to make the knot.

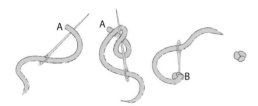

4 Seed Stitch and Double-Seed Stitch

Named because it gives the effect of a handful of seeds being scattered on the ground. The key is to make the stitches face in different directions. For variety I also like to work the double-seed stitch version. This little twist adds a small note of order to the randomness. Both these variations make a nice open (and quick!) filling stitch.

Bring the thread out at A and make a small straight stitch, inserting the needle at B. Then bring the needle out a short distance away and make another stitch of the same length at a different angle. Continue in this way to fill the area, trying to make your stitches as randomly placed as possible. To work a double seed, simply place pairs of stitches parallel to each other, but continue to place these double seeds in as many different directions as possible.

5 Running Stitch

This most basic of sewing stitches offers an interesting texture when worked in rows.

Working from right to left, bring the needle up to the right side of the work at A, then back down into the fabric a little way along the stitch line at B. Bring the needle out again about the same distance along at C. Repeat this action to form a line; use lines of running stitch to fill your shapes.

6 Split Stitch

This irregular filling stitch is like an overlapping backstitch. It gives a dense woven texture and can be used to fill larger areas than other solid stitches, such as satin stitch. For some reason I work my split stitch in the opposite direction to the orthodoxy, but it certainly works for me! Bring the needle up through the fabric at A, then back through at B, making a longer stitch then you would use for backstitch. Bring the needle up again at C, a half-stitch length away and bring down at D, in the center of the first stitch, splitting the fibers. Repeat with a few stitches in a row and then start to move in lines sideways, filling the space. This isn't such an exact stitch as the others; the idea is to get a nice even covering with no linen showing through.

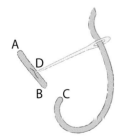

7 Bullion Knot

One of my favorite stitches, the bullion knot is very versatile and can be used as a filler or to add details to all sorts of embroidery designs. Bullion knots can have any number of thread wraps from two upward; the key is to match the number of wraps with the size of stitch (and the thickness of thread), which comes with practice. If your knot has a little hump and won't lie flat, then you need to make a longer stitch; and if you can see thread poking out at the ends of your knot, then your stitch is too long.

Bring your needle through at A and put it back through a stitch length away at B. The length of the stitch is dependent on the size of your bullion knot. Bring your needle out again at A, but *do not* pull your needle all the way through; instead, leave it halfway. Now start to wrap your thread around the tip of the needle. You may need to tilt the tip of the needle upward slightly to get these loops to stay on. Wrap the thread around the needle five or six times so that the coil of thread will cover the length of stitch. Place your thumb on the coiled thread and pull the needle through slowly and carefully so as not to disturb the coil. Insert the needle at B and gently pull the thread through until the bullion knot lies flat.

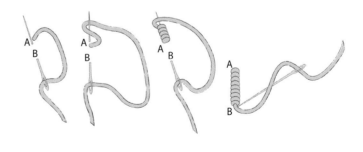

8 Laid Work

This name is rather a catch-all for a number of trellis-type crewelwork stitches that vary in degrees of intricacy. This is a simple couched version that adds a touch of Jacobean style while being able to retain a modern aesthetic. To give this stitch another modern twist, place your couching lines as vertical and horizontal rather than diagonal, which creates a square instead of the traditional diamond trellis, as in the Labyrinth Pouch (page 22).

Start by creating a grid over the chosen shape. Lay down all the threads that go in one direction first, placing your stitches just within the outline; then cross over the first layer with the second layer in the other direction. I always start with the center threads and work outward, lining up my stitches by eye. Using a contrasting thread, make tiny cross-stitches over the intersections of the laid threads, keeping your first and second stitches in the same order.

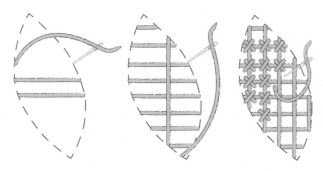

9 Cross-Stitch / Plus Stitch

Cross-stitch (or *plus stitch*) is one of the most basic stitches, but a very effective filler when used in rows. Bring the needle out at A and make a diagonal stitch to B, an equal distance up and to the left of A. Bring the needle out at C, immediately below A and level with B. Make another diagonal stitch in line with A and B to complete the stitch. For the plus stitch version, simply turn your stitch to the side so that the straight stitches are vertical and horizontal rather than diagonal.

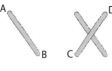

10 Star Stitch

Just one step up from cross-stitch. Start with a cross-stitch and add the star stitch on top by adding a vertical and a horizontal stitch.

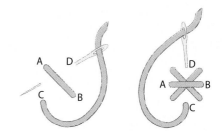

11 Felt Appliqué

The idea of using wool felt to fill some of the areas started with my first attempts at crewelwork. I simply thought that wool felt and wool threads belonged together. Mixing textures is a big part of this book, and using felt is a much quicker way to fill a space than embroidery, which is an added bonus. Save the felt appliqué option for your biggest areas and this will help you speed toward the finish line.

For the three projects that use this technique, I have prepared patterns for you to use to cut your felt. If you want to use this technique with other designs, simply trace the shape from the pattern to create your own template.

Tip When working "whipped" stitches, such as whipped backstitch, spiderweb, and woven rose, turn your needle around and insert through stitches with the eye end. This will stop you catching the fabric with the tip of the needle. Watch that sharp tip scratching the palm of your hand though!

Pin the felt in place and, using a matching thread, stitch to the fabric using small slip stitches that catch the edge of the felt. Don't place them too close to the edge, as this will shred your felt edges. Clover appliqué pins are helpful here as is Aurifil 80-weight thread, which is so fine it's almost invisible.

Felt appliqué

bonus stitches

12 Closed Herringbone Stitch (page 27)

13 Spiderweb Stitch (page 31)

14 Vintage Rose (page 37)

15 Lazy Daisy Stitch (page 40)

16 Fly Stitch (page 51)

17 Woven Rose (page 55)

18 Blanket Stitch (page 61)

19 Buttonhole Wheel (page 61)

20 Straight Stitch (page 87)

Doodle Hoop

A simple doodle is the perfect way to start our crewel embroidery journey. If you relax and take your pencil for a walk, you can draw interesting patterns full of intersecting curves that give three-dimensional effects. Filling these different shapes with our basic stitches creates fabulous texture. I've used all my favorite filling stitches plus this project's bonus stitch: closed herringbone. Feel free to create your own doodle or use mine, but fill it with your chosen stitches and colors.

Materials

FABRIC: 11″ × 11″ (28 × 28cm)
(I used Essex Linen Yarn-Dyed "Flax," a cotton/linen blend by Robert Kaufman Fabrics.)

TRANSFER PEN/PENCIL

WOODEN HOOP: 8″ (20cm)

THREAD: 1 each of Aurifil 12-weight wool 54-yard (50m) spools in the following colors:

A: black (8692)
B: peach (8212)
C: mint (8898)
D: yellow (8120)
E: raspberry red (8402)
F: cerise pink (8530)
G: magenta (8540)
H: white (8328)
I: blue (8810)
J: jade green (8870)

stitches

1 Chain (page 19): 2 strands

2 Satin (page 19): 2 strands

3 Colonial knot (page 20): 2 strands

4 Seed (page 20): 1 strand

5 Running (page 20): 1 strand

6 Split (page 21): 2 strands

12 Closed herringbone (bonus, page 27): 2 strands

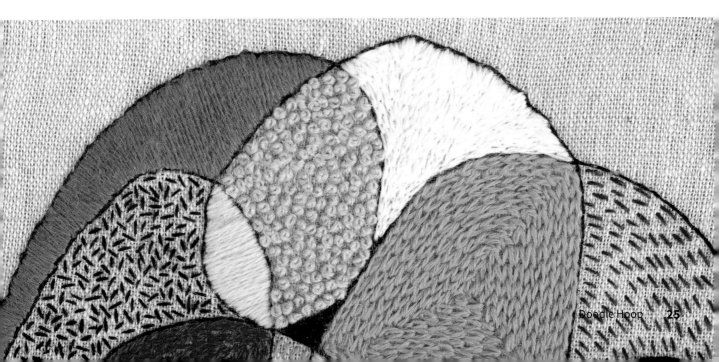

CONSTRUCTION

Preparation

Using the Doodle Hoop design pattern (page 92) and following the tracing instructions (see Tracing, page 13), trace the image onto the fabric. Insert the fabric in the hoop (see Hooping, page 15).

Stitching

1. Using backstitch and 1 strand of A black (8962), stitch all the outlines.

2. Following the stitch guide, fill each section with different stitches as shown.

Finishing

If necessary, remove the fabric from the hoop to erase any tracing lines and re-insert in the hoop. Follow the instructions to finish the hoop back (see Finishing a Hoop Back, page 16).

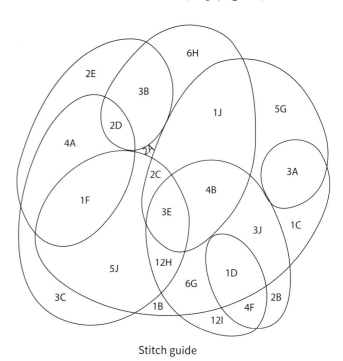

Stitch guide

Doodle hoop, close-up of texture

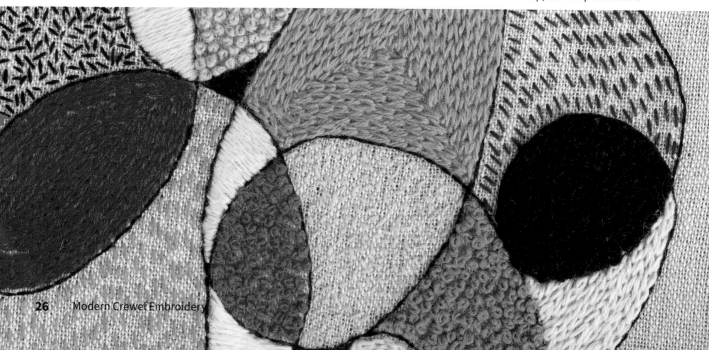

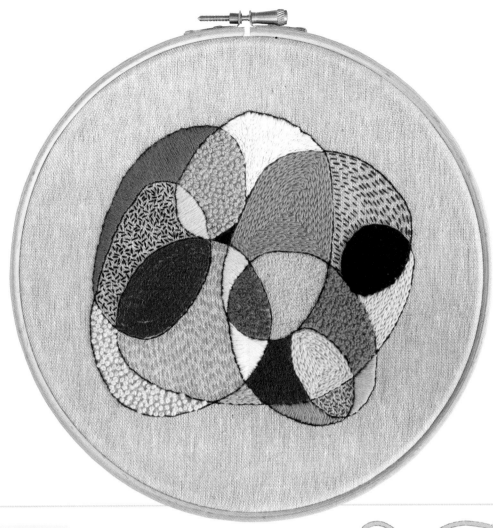

bonus stitch

12 *Closed Herringbone Stitch*

Closed herringbone is a variety of herringbone where the stitch is worked so closely together that it forms a line of crossed stitches. By varying the length of the stitches, it can be worked to fill a shape.

1. Bring the thread through at A and insert the needle diagonally down to the right at B.

2. Bring the thread through at C and insert the needle at D to make a cross.

3. Bring the thread through at E immediately beside A and insert the needle at F, beside B.

4. Bring the thread through at G, immediately beside C and insert the needle at H, beside D. Continue in this way to fill the shape, varying stitch lengths to fit.

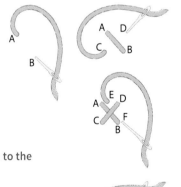

Labyrinth Pouch

Finished project: 8″ × 12″ (20 × 30.5cm) • **Stitched area:** 6″ × 9″ (15 × 23cm)

This square meandering design is based on one of my favorite free-motion quilting patterns. When I am not designing embroideries, I love to make quilts and I find my quilting inspires my embroidery designs and vice versa. As in the doodle hoop, your pencil or needle doesn't leave the piece but continues on a journey creating a sort of maze or labyrinth. Almost every other pattern in the book is created with curved lines, and there is a good reason for that, as stitching straight lines by hand is hard! But making this piece into a square pouch helps disguise rather than emphasize the "organic" straight lines. If you don't want to make a pouch, this would also work well as a framed picture, or try stretching it around a box canvas.

Materials

For embroidery:

FABRIC: 14″ × 23″ (35.5 × 58cm)
(I used Manchester Linen Yarn-Dyed "Pepper," a cotton/linen blend by Robert Kaufman Fabrics.)

TRANSFER PEN/PENCIL

WOODEN HOOP: 8″ (20cm)

THREAD: 1 each of Aurifil 12-weight wool 54-yard (50m) spools in the following colors:

Outline: white (8328)

A: peach (8212)

B: orange (8235)

C: dark orange (8242)

D: raspberry red (8402)

E: variegated orange (8003)

F: mint (8898)

G: jade green (8870)

H: sky blue (8823)

I: turquoise (8803)

J: variegated turquoise (8008)

K: dark blue (8730)

For pouch:

SEWING THREAD: To match Manchester Linen

ZIPPER: 12″ (30.5cm) nylon dress zipper

BACKING FABRIC: 1 strip 11″ × 13″ (28 × 33cm)
(I used Manchester Linen Yarn-Dyed "Pepper.")

LINING FABRIC: 2 strips 11″ × 13″ (28 × 33cm)

IRON-ON INTERFACING: 4 strips 11″ × 13″ (28 × 33cm)

ZIPPER END COVERS: 2 strips 1½″ × 2¾″ (4 × 7cm)

stitches

1. Chain (page 19): 2 strands
2. Satin (page 19): 2 strands
3. Colonial knot (page 20): 2 strands
4. Seed (page 20): 1 strand
5. Running (page 20): 1 strand
7. Bullion knot (page 21): 2 strands
8. Laid work (page 22): 1 strand
13. Spiderweb (bonus, page 31): 2 strands

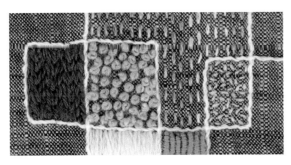

CONSTRUCTION

Preparation

Using the Labyrinth Pouch design pattern (page 93) and following the tracing instructions (see Tracing, page 13), trace the image onto the fabric. Insert the fabric in the hoop (see Hooping, page 15).

Stitching

1. Using a whipped backstitch and 1 strand of white (8328), stitch all the outlines.

2. Following the stitch guide, fill each section with different stitches as shown.

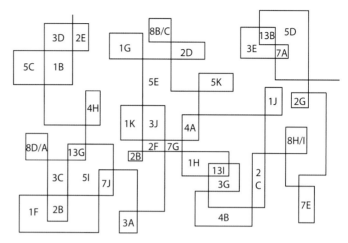

Stitch guide

Labyrinth pouch, close-up of texture

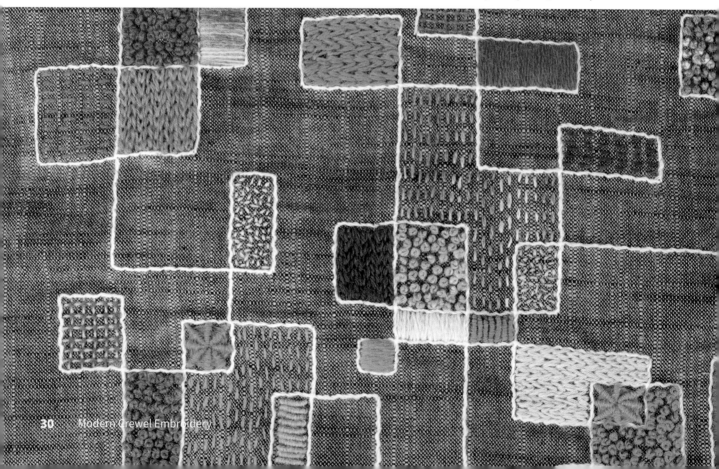

bonus stitch

13 *Spiderweb Stitch*

Other names for this stitch include Spiderweb Backstitch, Whipped Wheel Stitch, and many more. It can be used to fill small spaces as in this design or grouped together to fill larger areas. It has a wonderful raised texture that works perfectly with the wool thread.

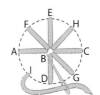

1. Bring the needle up at A and insert it at B, then bring the needle up at C and insert back in at B. Bring the needle up at D and then back in at B. Continue working alphabetically this way to make 8 spokes.

2. Bring the needle up just next to the middle of the wheel, between 2 spokes, such as C and G as shown. Pass the needle over and under spoke C and then under spoke G.

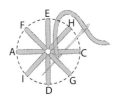

3. Next pass the needle over and under spoke G and then under spoke D.

4. Continue in this way around the wheel, passing the needle over and under a spoke and then under the adjacent one until the wheel is full. If you are using this stitch to fill an irregular shape, you may find some of your spokes are longer than others and require a few more wraps of thread to fill them.

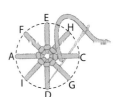

Make the Pouch

1. Remove the fabric from the hoop, remove any tracing lines, and press. Trim to 11″ × 13″ (28 × 33cm), centering the stitched design.

2. Carefully iron on the interfacing to the wrong side of both the front and back pouch outer pieces and lining fabric. To protect the embroidery, either press slowly with a low iron from the interfacing side or use a pressing cloth from the fabric side.

3. Finger press the fabric zipper end covers in half. Pin the covers to the zipper, right sides together, so that the raw edges overlap and line up with the zipper ends below. Topstitch the zipper end covers to either end of the zipper close to the fold line.

4. Put the outer fabric faceup. Place the zipper on top of this facedown, followed by the lining facedown. Pin it so that the top of the zipper and the top of the fabrics are all perfectly aligned; the zipper end covers will be slightly higher than the rest of this.

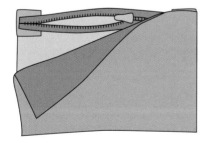

5. Pull the zipper open halfway. Attach a zipper foot to your sewing machine and sew close to the zipper, leaving about an ⅛″ (3mm) from the teeth. When you reach the zipper fastener, keep your needle down, raise the presser foot, and slide the zipper pull backward a little before carrying on sewing.

6. Flip the fabrics back to the right side and pin the remaining outer and lining fabric pieces to the other side of the zipper in exactly the same way as before. Sew this side of the zipper.

7. Press the outer and lining fabrics together, pulling them away from the zipper. Topstitch along either side of the zipper from the outer side.

8. Pull the zipper open halfway. Line the 2 pieces of outer fabric right sides together and do the same with the lining, making sure that the edges of the fabric all match up nicely. Now pin the linings together, making sure that the zipper ends are pointing downward into the lining side and not into the outer fabrics side. Check inside the seam to see that everything lines up.

9. Put the straight stitch foot back on the machine and use an approximate ⅜″ (9mm) seam. Start sewing one end of the lining base, about 3″ (7.5cm) from the corner. Sew all the way around the perimeter of the pouch until you get back to the lining base. Stop 3″ (7.5cm) after the corner to leave a gap for turning.

10. Flatten out the seams at each corner so the seams from base and sides touch (use a pin inserted through the center of the seam to make sure).

Using your ruler lined up on the seam, draw lines cutting across each corner at 1½˝ (4cm) from corner point. Sew along these lines. Trim away the corner, leaving a ¼˝ (6mm) seam.

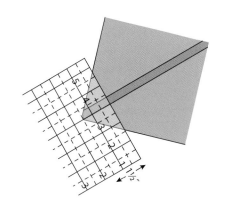

11. Turn inside out, pulling the main fabric through the lining. Push out the zipper ends with a poking tool. Turn under the seams at the lining gap, pin closed, and sew shut with a top stitch on the machine or hand sew using a neat slip stitch. Press both sides of the pouch gently. Push the lining inside the main fabric.

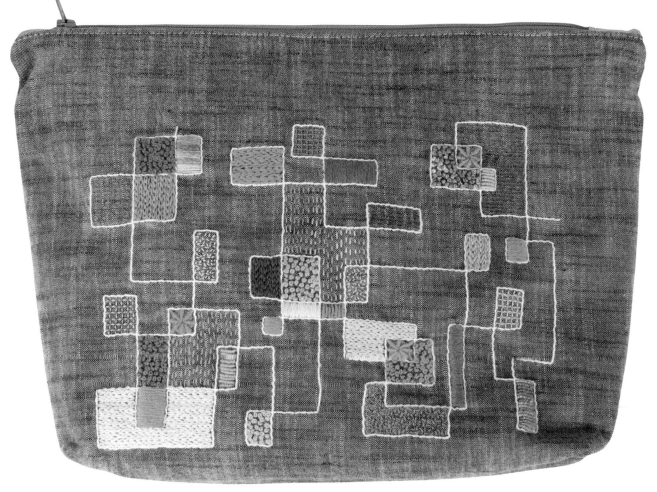

Bubbles Hoop

The original spark for this whole book was my Pebbles Sampler embroidery, which I made in 2019. Using wool thread and a wide variety of stitches created wonderful texture, especially when I added the felt appliqué details. I also enjoyed the mindful aspect of filling simple shapes with different stitches, and I have been planning to make another one ever since I finished the original. For this new version, I have concentrated on simple round bubble shapes and used a restricted palette of blues and greens to give an aquatic feel. The cotton fabric is a hand-dyed cotton, which gives extra movement to the piece.

Materials

FABRIC: 10″ × 10″ (25 × 25cm)
(I used Hand-Dyed Osnaburg in "Light Ocean," a cotton fabric with a linen-like texture by Fiber on a Whim.)

TRANSFER PEN/PENCIL

WOODEN HOOP: 7″ (17.5cm)

WOOL FELT SCRAPS: Green / blue / turquoise shades

THREAD: 1 each of Aurifil 12-weight wool 54-yard (50m) spools in the following colors:

Outline: charcoal (8083)

A: dark green (8890)

B: sky blue (8805)

C: mint (8898)

D: jade green (8875)

E: leaf green (8962)

F: grass green (8965)

G: teal (8870)

H: variegated green (8007)

I: pale turquoise (8823)

J: dark blue (8735)

K: pale green (8860)

L: pale yellow (8112)

M: variegated blue (8009)

N: variegated turquoise (8008)

O: turquoise (8803)

stitches

1. Chain (page 19): 2 strands
2. Satin (page 19): 2 strands
3. Colonial knot (page 20): 2 strands
4. Seed (page 20): 1 strand
8. Laid work (page 22): 2 strands
10. Star (page 22): 1 strand
11. Felt appliqué (page 23): 2 strands
13. Spiderweb (bonus, page 31): 2 strands
14. Vintage rose (bonus, page 37): 2 strands

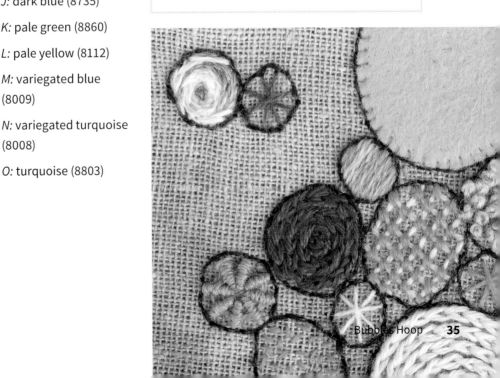

CONSTRUCTION

Preparation

Using the Bubbles Hoop design pattern (page 94) and following the tracing instructions (see Tracing, page 13), trace the image onto the fabric. Insert the fabric in the hoop (see Hooping, page 15).

Stitching

1. Using backstitch and 1 strand of charcoal (8083), stitch all the outlines except those around the felt appliqué (#11) circles.

2. Following the stitch guide, fill each section with different stitches as shown.

3. Using the Bubbles Hoop bubbles/circles appliqué patterns (page 95), cut out 6 different felt bubbles/circles. Pin in place over the matching circles and stitch down with matching thread (see Felt Appliqué, page 23). Using 1 strand of charcoal (8083), stitch the outlines around the felt.

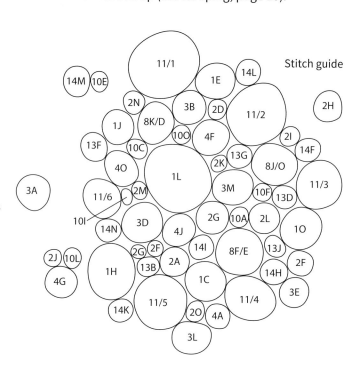

Stitch guide

Finishing

If necessary, remove the fabric from the hoop to erase any tracing lines and re-insert in the hoop. Follow the instructions to finish the hoop back (see Finishing a Hoop Back, page 16).

Bubbles hoop, close-up of texture

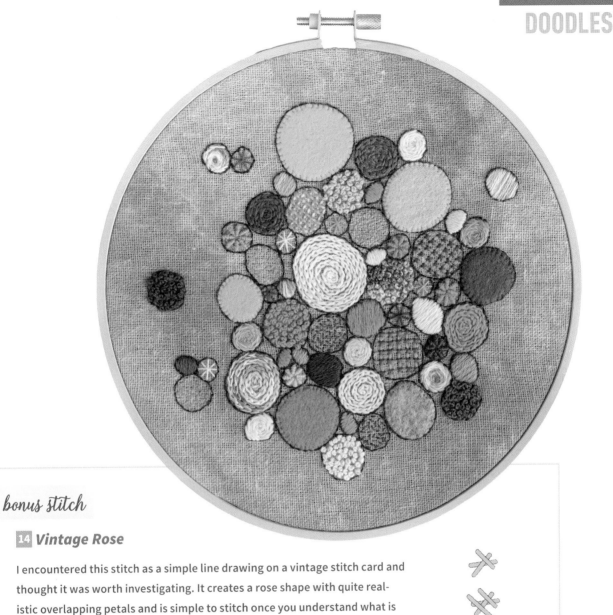

bonus stitch

14 *Vintage Rose*

I encountered this stitch as a simple line drawing on a vintage stitch card and thought it was worth investigating. It creates a rose shape with quite realistic overlapping petals and is simple to stitch once you understand what is required. I teach this stitch often and advise my students to "Imagine the rose, and the rose will appear," and that seems to do the trick!

1. Begin by making 3 small straight stitches in a rough triangle shape with overlapping corners.

2. Next make a ring of straight stitches around the triangle, crossing the corners and building up more sides. Bring the needle up alongside and at the middle of each stitch and lay the next stitch at a slight angle so that each stitch overlaps the one before and softens any edge points.

3. Keep working outward in this way. The outline will become more rounded as it gets bigger, and a rose will emerge as if by magic! If you are filling an irregular shape, continue overlapping into the spaces at empty corners.

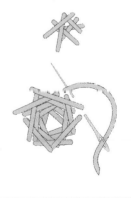

Shapes Pincushion Trio

Finished project: 2½″ × 4¾″ (6.5 × 12cm) each • **Stitched area:** 1½″ × 4″ (4 × 10cm)

Appletons crewel wool is where my love of crewel embroidery began while working on The Great Tapestry of Scotland (page 7), so I had to include a little of it in this book. My first craft business was designing needlepoint kits, and I used Appletons tapestry wool for all my designs. Many of the shade numbers must have become embedded in my brain as they seemed already familiar when I started choosing threads for this project, with the luscious red (502) being a particular old favorite. This is a nice quick project, using the simplest shapes I could draw and with the thicker weight of thread filling the shapes with speed. Why three pincushions though? Things always look better in three, especially when they are tiny and each is in a different colorway. And in my experience, you can never have too many pincushions!

Materials

FABRIC: 11″ × 18″ (28 × 45.5cm)
(I used Essex Linen Yarn-Dyed "Black," a cotton/linen blend by Robert Kaufman Fabrics.)

TRANSFER PEN/PENCIL

WOODEN HOOP: 8″ (20cm)

POLYESTER FIBERFILL: For toy filling

SEWING THREAD: To match Essex Linen

THREAD: 1 each of Appletons Crewel Wool 25m (27.3 yards) skeins in the following colors:

Outline: white (991)

A: pink (801)

B: magenta (803)

C: purple (454)

D: green (434)

E: turquoise (483)

F: pale green (423)

G: orange (441)

H: dark orange (445)

I: red (502)

stitches

1. Chain (page 19): 1 strand
2. Satin (page 19): 2 strands
3. Colonial knot (page 20): 1 strand
4. Seed (page 20): 1 strand
5. Running (page 20): 1 strand
6. Split (page 21): 2 strands
7. Bullion knot (page 21): 2 strands
8. Laid work (page 22): 1 strand
9. Lazy daisy (bonus, page 40): 1 strand

CONSTRUCTION

Preparation

From the Essex Linen, cut a square 11″ × 11″ (28 × 28cm) for the embroidery. Set aside the remainder for the pincushion backs.

Using the Shapes Pincushion Trio pattern (page 96) and following the tracing instructions (see Tracing, page 13), trace the image onto the fabric. Insert the fabric in the hoop (see Hooping, page 15).

Stitching

1. Using backstitch and 1 strand of white (991), stitch all the outlines.

2. Following the stitch guide, fill each section with different stitches as shown.

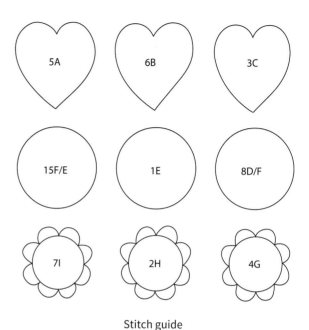

Stitch guide

---

bonus stitch

15 *Lazy Daisy Stitch*

Probably the cutest stitch there is and perennially popular, this is simply a group of detached chain stitches worked in a circle to create a flower shape. In some of the designs in this book, I've either left the center of the flower empty or, like here, added a single colonial knot in a contrast thread. I usually work my flowers with 6 petals, but 5 will do if you are running out of space (or thread!).

1. Bring the needle up at A and down at B, as close to A as possible.

2. Bring the needle up at C and loop the thread around the needle, or make sure the needle is on top of the stitch loop at you bring it through.

3. Insert the needle at D, passing the thread over the loop catching it down.

4. Make another stitch beside this one but at a slight angle.

5. Continue to place your petal stitches in a circle to complete the flower. Try not to pull your petals too tight or they will close up.

Simple shapes trio, close-up of texture

Make Pincushions

1. Remove embroidery from hoop, remove any tracing lines, and press.

2. Trim each embroidery to give you 3 strips 3″ × 5½″ (7.5 × 14cm), centering each motif. From the remaining Essex linen, cut 3 strips 3″ × 5½″ (7.5 × 14cm) for the backs.

3. Pin a front to a back, right sides together. Using a ¼″ (6mm) seam allowance, machine stitch all the way around, leaving a 2½″ (6.5cm) gap along the bottom edge. Snip a little off the corners within the seam allowance. Turn it inside out and stuff firmly. Turn under the edges at the opening and pin together. Stitch closed by hand using a tiny, neat ladder stitch or whipstitch.

Tip If you want to make this entirely by hand, you can sew around your pincushions using a backstitch or a tiny running stitch.

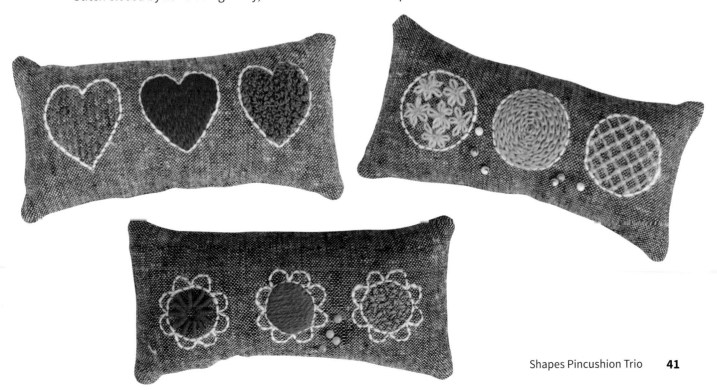

Shapes Pincushion Trio   **41**

Loops Stitch Booklet

Finished project: 3″ × 4″ (7.5 × 10cm) • **Stitched area:** 8″ × 12″ (20 × 30.5cm)

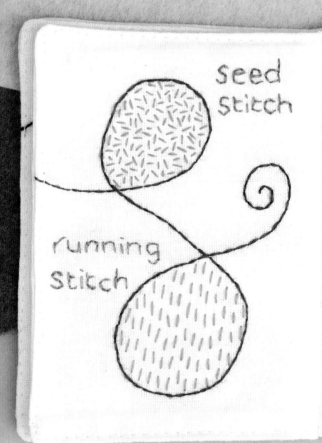

Now that you've had a chance to try them out, let's mark and celebrate our favorite stitches with this super-cute stitch book! It even has a neat space for storing your needles at the back. Just in case you ever forget these basic stitches, this handy little fabric booklet will be there to guide you. The loop design is another one that is inspired by my free-motion quilting practice, with the loops taking you from page to page all the way to the needles. Feel free to personalize the text and stitches used throughout.

Materials

FABRIC: 12″ × 18″ (30.5 × 45.5cm)
(I used Essex Linen "Bleached White," a cotton/linen blend by Robert Kaufman Fabrics.)

FELT: 2″ × 2½″ (5 × 6.5cm)

TRANSFER PEN/PENCIL

WOODEN HOOP: 7″ (18cm)

THREAD: 1 each of Aurifil 12-weight wool 54-yard (50m) spools in the following colors:

Outline: charcoal (8083)

Text: gray (8609)

A: cerise pink (8530)

B: pale green (8860)

C: sky blue (8803)

D: magenta (8540)

E: mauve (8535)

F: jade green (8875)

G: egg yolk (8135)

H: turquoise (8803)

I: orange (8235)

stitches

1 Chain (page 19): 2 strands

2 Satin (page 19): 2 strands

3 Colonial knot (page 20): 2 strands

4 Seed (page 20): 1 strand

5 Running (page 20): 1 strand

6 Split (page 21): 2 strands

7 Bullion knot (page 21): 2 strands

8 Laid work (page 22): 2 strands

13 Spiderweb (bonus, page 31): 2 strands

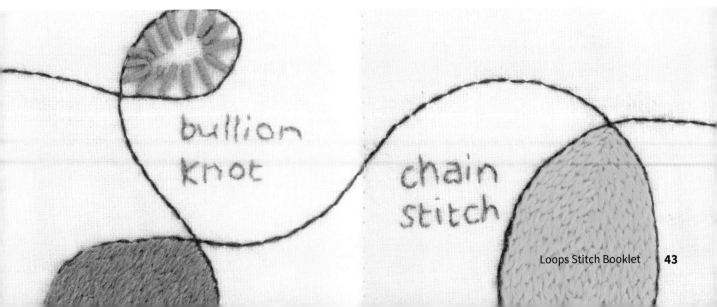

bullion knot

chain stitch

CONSTRUCTION

Preparation

Using the 2 Loops Stitch Booklet patterns (pages 97 and 98) and following the tracing instructions (see Tracing, page 13), trace the image onto the fabric (including outline). Insert the fabric in the hoop (see Hooping, page 15).

Stitching

1. Using backstitch and 1 strand of charcoal (8083), stitch all the outlines.

2. Using backstitch and 2 strands of gray (8609), stitch all the text.

3. Following the stitch guide, fill each section with different stitches as shown.

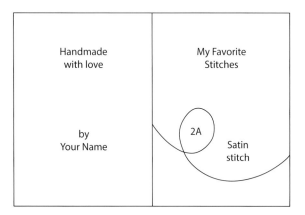

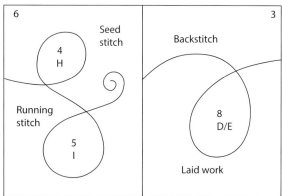

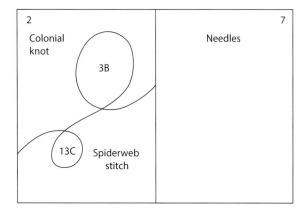

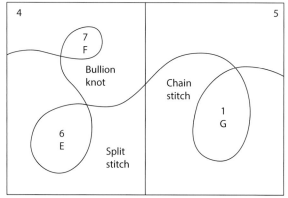

Stitch guides

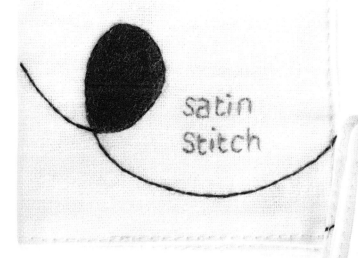

Loops stitch booklet, close-up of texture

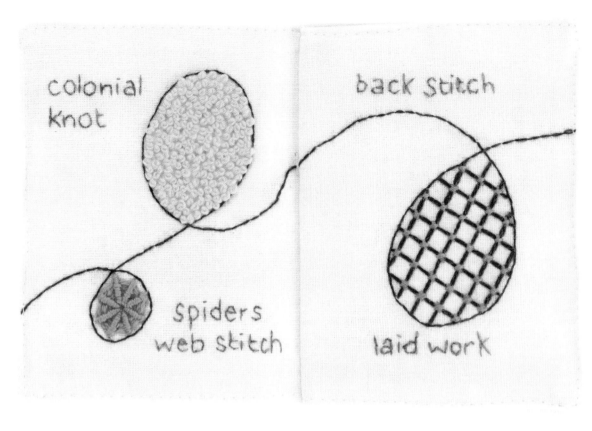

colonial knot

back stitch

spiders web stitch

laid work

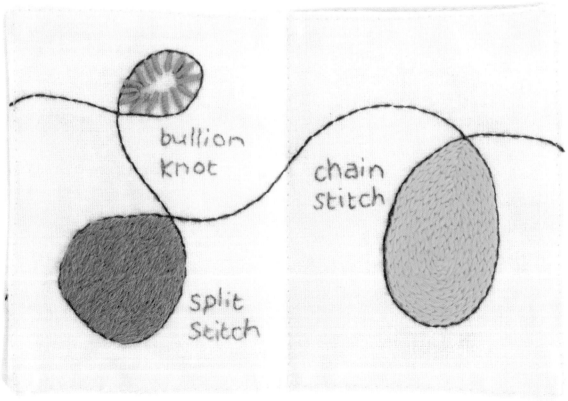

bullion knot

chain stitch

split stitch

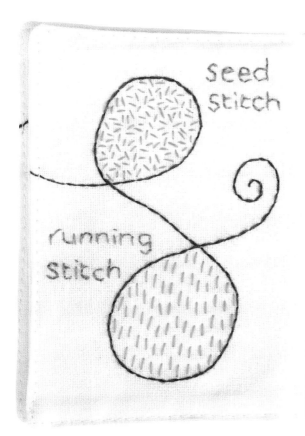
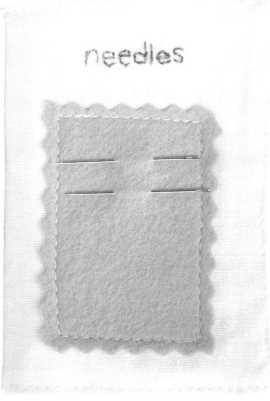

Making the Booklet

1. Remove the fabric from the hoop and trim each double page to a 4½″ × 6½″ (11.5 × 16.5cm) strip, taking care to center the stitching. Press or wash to remove any tracing lines.

2. Pin the felt piece to the empty *page 7* area and sew it in place by stitching around the edge, either by hand or machine.

3. Place *pages 1/8* (cover and back) and *pages 2/7* right sides together and pin. Stitch a ¼″ (6mm) seam around the outside, leaving a 2½″ (6.5cm) gap in center of the bottom edge. Snip a little excess from the corners within the seam allowance. Turn it inside out. Turn under the seam allowance at the opening and press. Sew all the way around the edge, using a neat top stitch, closing the gap as you go.

4. Repeat with *pages 3/6* and *pages 4/5*. Place these pages on top of previous pages and fold them in half. Press. Stitch along the pressed center line from the outside of the book (*pages 1/8*).

Scandi Fish Hoop

Finished project: 6″ × 9″ (15 × 23cm) • **Stitched area:** 4″ × 5″ (10 × 12.5cm)

Inspired by a small tray bought in Stockholm, this design celebrates the simple yet effective graphic design of the Scandinavian countries that has been so successfully exported to the rest of the world. This reminds me of the simple samplers I made as a schoolgirl, with rows of cross and fly stitches filling the line spaces and creating the pattern. But the fish motif is a little more fun and the charcuterie hoop by Auburn Hoops makes the perfect frame for this whimsical dish. It is also the sort of project that can be finished in a day.

Materials

FABRIC: 10″ × 11″ (25.5 × 28cm)
(I used Essex Linen Yarn-Dyed "Cadet," a cotton/linen blend by Robert Kaufman Fabrics.)

TRANSFER PEN/PENCIL

WOODEN HOOP: 7″ (18cm)

THREAD: 1 each of Aurifil 12-weight wool 54-yard (50m) spools in the following colors:

Outline: indigo (8092)

A: red (8258)

B: raspberry red (8402)

C: variegated orange (8003)

D: peach (8212)

E: white (8328)

F: variegated brown (8012)

G: yellow (8120)

H: blue (8742)

I: pale yellow (8115)

J: pale blue (8757)

K: dark blue (8780)

stitches

1 Chain (page 19): 2 strands

2 Satin (page 19): 2 strands

3 Colonial knot (page 20): 2 strands

9 Cross (page 22): 1 strand

16 Fly (bonus, page 51): 1 strand

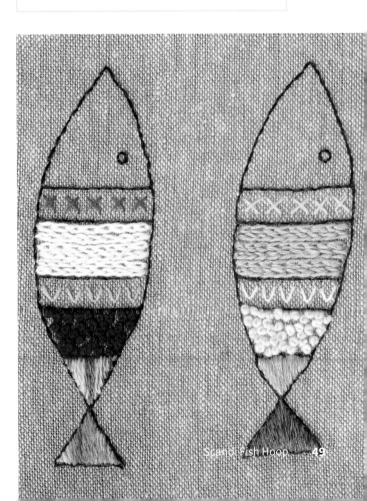

CONSTRUCTION

Preparation

Using the Scandi Fish Hoop pattern (page 99) and following the tracing instructions (see Tracing, page 13), trace the image onto the fabric. Insert the fabric in the hoop (see Hooping, page 15).

Stitching

1. Using backstitch and 1 strand of indigo (8092), stitch all the outlines.

2. Following the stitch guide, fill each section with different stitches as shown.

Finishing

If necessary, remove the fabric from the circular stitching hoop to erase any tracing lines and insert into the special oval hoop. Follow the instructions to finishing the hoop back (see Finishing a Hoop Back, page 16).

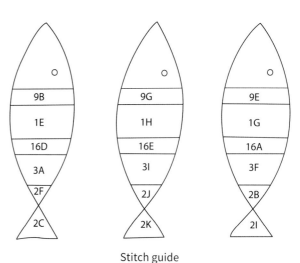

Stitch guide

Scandi fish, close-up of texture

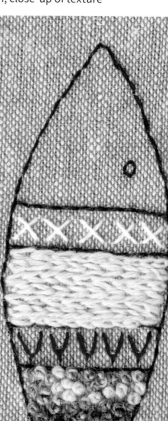

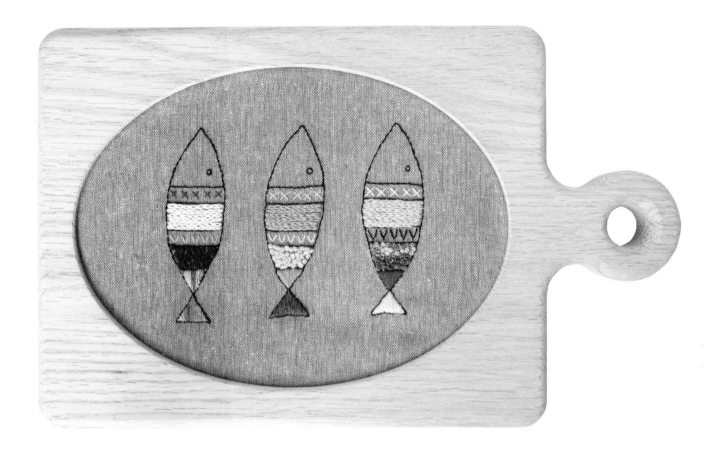

bonus stitch

16 *Fly Stitch*

This simple V-shape stitch looks good worked in rows but can be adapted to fill shapes, as in the curved rows used in the Clamshell Pillow (page 88).

1. Bring the needle up at A and down at B, but don't pull the thread tight; instead, leave a small loop.

2. Bring the needle up at C where you want the point of the V to be and loop it over the stitch you made between A and B.

3. Pull the thread and place your needle at D so that you catch down the V point to complete the stitch.

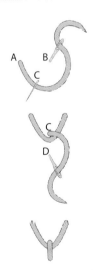

Arts and Crafts Tree Wallhanging

Finished project: 13½″ × 16″ (34 × 40.5cm) • **Stitched area:** 9″ × 9½″ (23 × 24cm)

As I mentioned in the introduction, one of my first embroidery designs was of a sampler tree with different stitches grouped together along the branches. For this book, I've created a new version of a tree sampler that uses large rounded leaf shapes instead, filling each leaf with different stitches. Something about the shape of the leaf and the espaliered branches made me think of the Arts and Crafts Movement of the late nineteenth century. Finishing the hanging with a tabard top emphasizes the antique style. I chose rich autumn colors for the leaves, which give a strong contrast with the frog green linen.

Materials

FABRIC: 17″ × 20″ (43 × 51cm)
(I used Cashel 3281 28-count Linen, "Grass Green" shade 6130, by Zweigart.)

FELT SCRAPS: Orange and red shades

IRON-ON INTERFACING: 2 squares
13½″ × 13½″ (34 × 34cm)

LINING FABRIC: 17″ × 20″ (43 × 51cm)
(I used Manchester Linen Yarn-Dyed "Leaf," a cotton/linen blend by Robert Kaufman Fabrics.)

TRANSFER PEN/PENCIL

WOODEN HOOP: 10″ (25cm)

THREAD: 1 each of Aurifil 12-weight wool 54-yard (50m) spools in the following colors:

Outline: dark brown (8361)

A: raspberry red (8402)

B: dull orange (8215)

C: egg yolk (8135)

D: dark orange (8260)

E: variegated orange (8003)

F: red (8258)

G: orange (8242)

H: yellow (8120)

I: pale apricot (8205)

J: variegated dark red (8089)

K: pale orange (8235)

L: variegated brown (8012)

stitches

1. Chain (page 19): 2 strands
2. Satin (page 19): 2 strands
3. Colonial knot (page 20): 2 strands
4. Seed (page 20): 2 strands
5. Running (page 20): 2 strands
6. Split (page 21): 2 strands
8. Laid work (page 22): 2 strands
11. Felt appliqué (page 23)
15. Lazy daisy (bonus, page 40): 1 strand
17. Woven rose (bonus, page 55): 2 strands

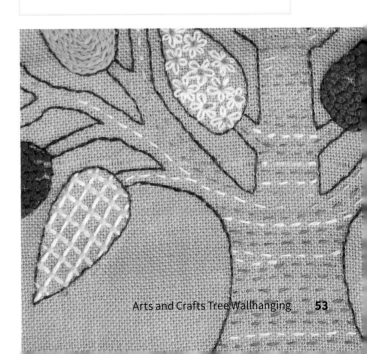

Arts and Crafts Tree Wallhanging   **53**

CONSTRUCTION

Preparation

From the Zweigart linen, cut a square 16″ × 16″ (41 × 41cm) for the embroidery. Set aside the reminder for the wallhanging.

Using the Arts and Crafts Tree Wallhanging tree pattern (page 100) and following the tracing instructions (see Tracing, page 13), trace the image onto the fabric. Insert the fabric in the hoop (see Hooping, page 15).

Stitching

1. Using backstitch and 1 strand of dark brown (8361), stitch all the outlines except those around the felt appliqué (#11) leaves.

2. Following the stitch guide, fill each section with different stitches as shown.

3. For the satin stitch areas, stitch a vertical line of backstitch in one of the colors, filling half of the leaf with this color and slanting satin stitches. Fill the other side in the same way with the other color indicated.

4. Using the Arts and Crafts Tree Wallhanging leaf appliqué pattern (page 101), cut out 3 felt leaves. Pin in place over each #11 shape indicated in the stitch guide and stitch down with matching thread (see Felt Appliqué, page 23). Using 1 strand of dark brown (8361), stitch the outlines around the felt.

5. Fill the tree trunk with vertical lines of running stitch, using a single strand of variegated brown (8012). Fill the tree branches with lines of running stitch as shown.

Stitch guide

bonus stitch

17 Woven Rose

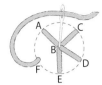

Also known as a spiderweb rose, I call this a woven rose to distinguish it from the vintage rose. This is the more popular of the 2 roses and is very prevalent in modern designs. As with the spiderweb, this can be used to fill a small space in its entirety or individual roses can be grouped together.

1. Bring the needle up at A and insert it at B, then bring the needle up at C and insert back at B. Continue this way to create 5 spokes.

2. Bring the needle up just next to the middle of the wheel and weave the thread over and under each spoke.

3. Keep going in this way to completely cover the spokes. Finish by bringing the needle to the back.

Arts and crafts tree, close-up of texture

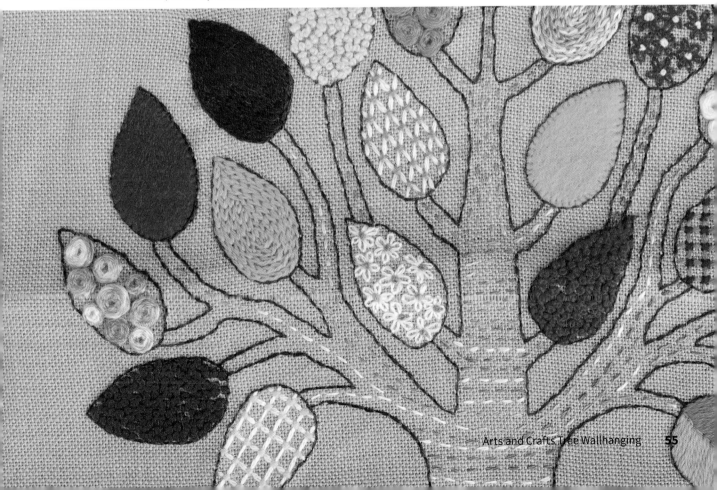

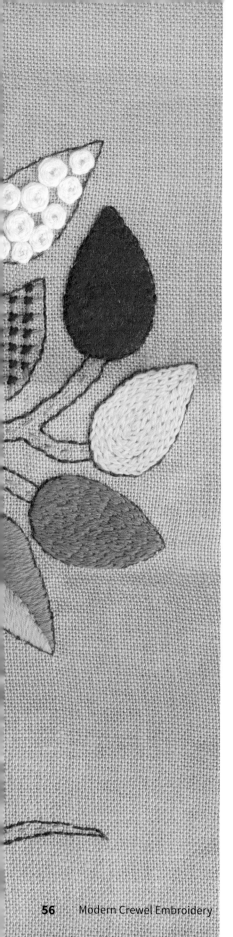

Finishing

1. Remove from the hoop to erase any tracing lines; trim to a square 14″ × 14″ (35.5 × 35.5cm).

2. From the remaining linen, cut 3 strips 3½″ × 5½″ (9 × 14cm) for the tabs. From the lining fabric, cut 1 square 14″ × 14″ (35.5 × 35.5cm) for the back of the embroidery and 3 strips 3½″ × 5½″ (9 × 14cm) for the tabs.

3. Carefully iron the interfacing to the wrong side of both the embroidery front and lining back. To protect the embroidery, either press slowly with a low iron from the interfacing side or use a pressing cloth from the fabric side.

4. Place the main and lining tab strips right sides together and stitch a ¼″ (6mm) seam along both long sides. Turn it inside out and press. Using a neat top stitch, sew close to the edge of both seams.

5. Press the 3 tabs in half so the raw edges meet and the lining sides face each other.

6. Pin along the top edge of the embroidery with right sides together, leaving a 1″ (2.5cm) space free at either end of the embroidery and a 1½″ (4cm) space between each tab. Sew a basting stitch ⅛″ (3mm) from the top to secure the tabs.

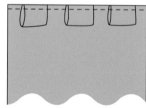

Attach tabs to top of wallhanging with basting stitch.

7. Place the lining right sides together with the embroidery, so that the tabs are sandwiched between. Using a ¼″ (6mm) seam, start sewing along the bottom edge 4″ (10cm) from the corner. Sew all the way around, stopping 4″ (10cm) from the opposite corner, leaving an opening. Snip the corners within the seam allowance, turn right side out, and press. Sew a neat top stitch all the way around, closing the opening as you go.

8. Insert a wooden dowel or tree branch through the tabs to hang onto the wall.

Sea Urchin Pincushion

Finished project (w × h × d): 4″ × 2″ × 4″ (10 × 5 × 10cm)
Stitched area: 3¾″ × 3¾″ (9.5 × 9.5cm)

I have been making a patchwork version of this abstract sea urchin design for a while now. I usually embellish it with embroidery, beads, and buttons to create a large pincushion/paperweight shape. But here you will use just embroidery and stitch onto felt, using it as a background rather than to fill spaces. Try to get 100% wool felt, if possible, or felt with the most wool content you can find. It is a very tactile, stable material and therefore doesn't need to be placed in a hoop. You can also leave your knots in place on the back of the felt. Using felt means you can use a blanket stitch for seams and not have to worry about raw edges and turning the pincushion inside out, so the construction is very simple. I have chosen pale pastel shades that remind me of seashells.

Materials

PALE GRAY WOOL FELT: 1 rectangle 9″ × 14″ (23 × 35.5cm)

TRACING WHEEL

TRANSFER PEN/PENCIL

POLYESTER FIBERFILL: For toy stuffing

CARD STOCK: 1 square 4½″ × 4½″ (11.4 × 11.4cm)

THREAD: 1 each of Aurifil 12-weight wool 54-yard (50m) spools in the following colors:

Outline and blanket stitch edging: brown (8910)

A: brown (8320)

B: pale green (8898)

C: variegated pink (8006)

D: mauve (8553)

E: pale pink (8425)

F: pink (8464)

G: yellow (8130)

H: orange (8215)

I: variegated orange (8002)

stitches

1 Chain (page 19): 2 strands

3 Colonial knot (page 20): 2 strands

5 Running (page 20): 1 strand

7 Bullion knot (page 21): 2 strands

9 Cross (page 22): 1 strand

10 Star (page 22): 1 strand

15 Lazy daisy (bonus, page 40): 1 strand

17 Woven rose (bonus, page 55): 2 strands

18 Blanket (bonus, page 61): 1 strand

19 Buttonhole wheel (bonus, page 61): 1 strand

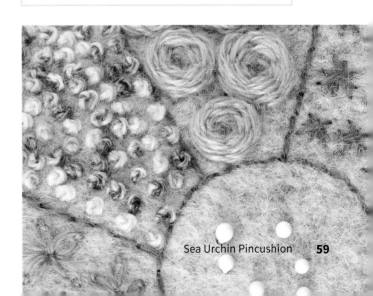

Sea Urchin Pincushion   **59**

CONSTRUCTION

Preparation

From the wool felt, cut a square 7″ × 7″ (17.5 × 17.5cm). Using the Sea Urchin Pincushion top/bottom pattern (page 101) and following the tracing instructions (see Tracing, page 13), mark the image onto the felt with the tracing wheel and marking pen. (*Note:* There is no need to use a hoop when working with felt.)

Stitching

1. Using backstitch and 1 strand of brown (8910), stitch all the outlines.

2. Following the stitch guide, fill each section with different stitches as shown.

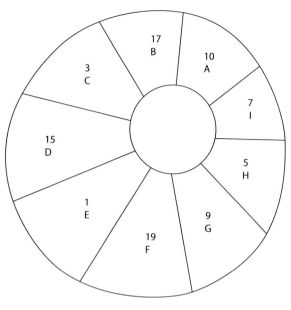

Stitch guide

Sea urchin pincushion, close-up of texture

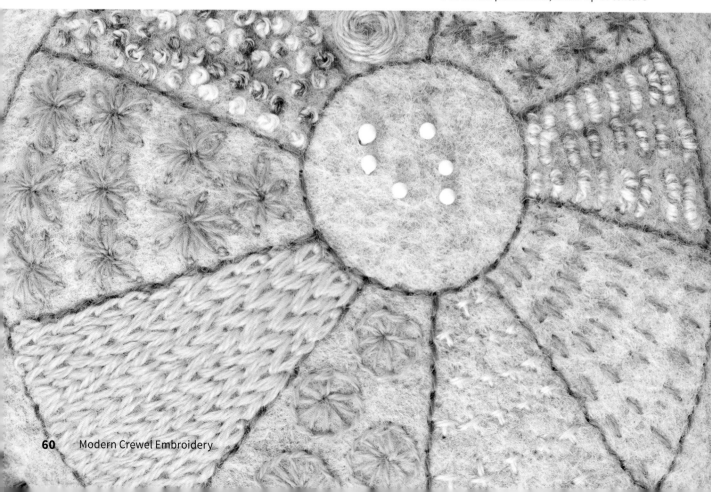

bonus stitches

These 2 stitches are basically the same action but with one worked in a line and the wheel worked in a circle.

18 Blanket Stitch

Blanket stitch is a traditional stitch, used for binding and finishing the edges of a wool blanket. It can also be used as a way of joining pieces, as here, or as a decorative outline.

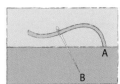

1. With the 2 pieces of felt together bring the needle out from between the pieces and through the felt on one side at A. Loop it over the felt edges and in again at B and back through to the first side at C, catching the loop of thread with the tip of the needle and pulling through to make the first stitch.

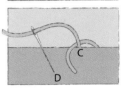

2. Continue with the next stitch, bringing your thread over the felt edges and in at D and out again at E on the other side, catching the loop with your needle. Try to leave an even space between each stitch.

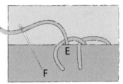

19 Buttonhole Wheel

When blanket stitch is used for a hand buttonhole, it is called buttonhole stitch, or as here, to make these sweet little wheels. This is another stitch that looks good grouped together as a filler. You always need to be firm and taut with this stitch as it is easy to "turn over" the edge stitches unless you keep an adequate stitch tension, though even if this happens, your wheels will still look cute.

1. Bring the needle up at A and down at B, but don't pull the thread tight; instead, leave a small loop.

2. Bring the needle up at C, making sure it's inside the loop; you can use your finger to hold it in place.

3. Insert the needle at B and bring it out at D to create the next spoke. Continue in this way to create the wheel.

4. Finish with a tiny stitch joining at A.

Finishing

1. Erase any tracing lines by the recommended method and gently press.

2. Using the Sea Urchin Pincushion card insert pattern (page 101), cut a circle from card stock.

3. From the remaining wool felt, cut a strip 1½″ × 13½″ (4 × 34cm) for the pincushion sides.

4. Using the Sea Urchin Pincushion top/bottom pattern (page 101) and centering the embroidery, cut out the pincushion top. Using the same pattern and the remaining felt, cut out the pincushion bottom.

5. Pin the side strip around the embroidered top, wrong sides together. Start to blanket stitch around the edge, leaving ³⁄₁₆″ (5mm) of felt free on the side strip before your first stitch. Stitch all the way around before joining the 2 side ends and stitch along these.

6. Pin the felt bottom to the other edge of the side strip and blanket stitch just over halfway around. Insert the card base and start to carefully stuff the pincushion. Continue stitching around and carefully adding more filling until pincushion is stuffed. Close the gap with last few stitches.

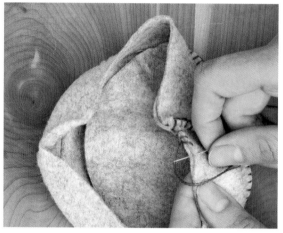

Sewing the pincushion with blanket stitch

Tip For a heavier weight to your pincushion, place a small plastic ziplock bag full of rice in the bottom along with the toy filling.

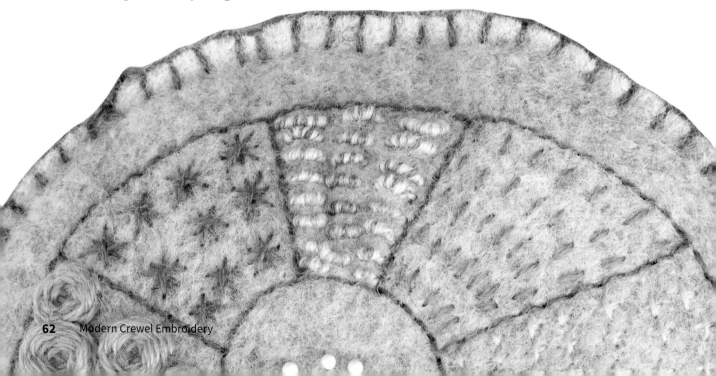

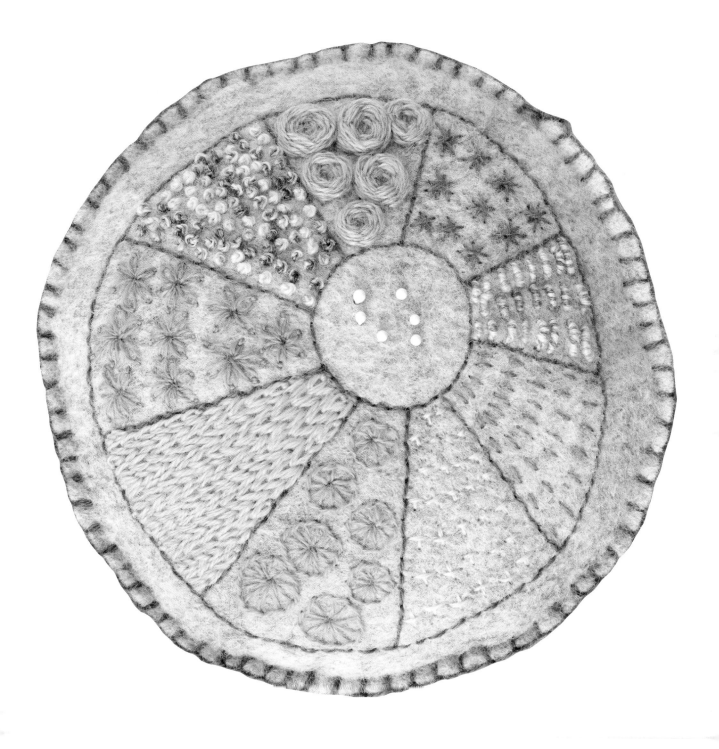

Sea Urchin Pincushion **63**

Tendrils Pot

Finished project (w × h × d): 5″ × 5½″ × 5″ (12.5 × 14 × 12.5cm)
Stitched area: 5″ × 17″ (12.5 × 43cm)

I love the way a simple leaf shape can be used to make a graphic geometric design. This classic motif can be seen on all sorts of home furnishings and ceramics, and I decided to create my own texture-filled fabric pot as a soft, cozy homage. I've kept the colors in line for a uniform, ordered look. To compliment the Scandi feel, I've paired the design with vintage Swedish linen threads that can still be bought online (see Resources, page 109). As they are from a wide variety of manufacturers, I have not included the shade numbers.

This design would look just as good stitched in regular cotton floss, with one strand of the linen being approximately two of the floss. The linen thread is thick and lustrous but is a little harder on the hands than the wool. Strictly speaking, using linen rather than wool means this design cannot be called crewel embroidery, but the temptation to play with different threads proved too strong for me to care much about that! This would make a fabulous rectangular embroidered picture if you don't want a pot, perhaps stretched over a box canvas. But if you do want to make a useful storage pot and have any old unwanted CDs, they work perfectly for the base!

Materials

For embroidery:

FABRIC: 10″ × 19″ (25 × 48cm)
(I used Belfast 3609 32-count Linen, "Raw" shade 53, by Zweigart.)

TRANSFER PEN/PENCIL

WOODEN HOOP: 7″ (18cm)

THREAD: 1 each of linen thread or cotton floss skeins in the following colors:

Outline: dark brown	*E:* hot pink
A: aqua	*F:* pale pink
B: purple	*G:* green
C: pale green	*H:* pale orange
D: orange	*I:* dark green

For fabric pot:

FABRIC: 1 strip 13″ × 18″ (33 × 46cm) for base and lining
(I used Sevenberry Canvas Cotton, SB-W8067D1-3 Aqua, by Sevenberry for Robert Kaufman Fabrics.)

IRON-ON INTERFACING: 1 strip 5″ × 17″ (13 × 43cm) and 1 strip 6″ × 17″ (15 × 43cm)

BATTING: 2 squares 6″ × 6″ (15 × 15cm)

CARD STOCK: 1 square 6″ × 6″ (15 × 15cm), or use an old CD!

GLUE STICK

CONSTRUCTION

Preparation

Using the Tendrils Pot side pattern (page 102) and following the tracing instructions (see Tracing, page 13), trace the image onto the fabric. Insert the fabric in the hoop (see Hooping, page 15).

Stitching

1. Using backstitch and 1 strand of dark brown, stitch all the outlines.

2. Following the stitch guide, fill each section with different stitches as shown. Use 1 strand of linen thread for all stitches.

3. For the satin stitch areas, stitch a vertical line of backstitch in one of the colors, filling half of the leaf with this color and slanting satin stitches. Fill the other side in the same way with the other color indicated.

4. Work short horizontal satin stitches in aqua to fill the stems.

Tendrils pot, close-up of texture

Stitch guide

Making the Pot

1. Remove the fabric from the hoop, erase any tracing lines, and press. Trim to 5½″ × 17½″ (14 × 44.5cm), making sure there is at least a ¼″ (6mm) seam allowance at the top and bottom edges of the embroidery and centering the motif side to side.

2. From the lining fabric, cut a strip 6″ × 17½″ (15 × 44.5cm). Using the Tendrils Pot base pattern (page 103), cut 2 circles from the lining fabric. Using the Tendrils Pot card insert pattern (page 104), cut 1 circle from card stock (unless you are using an old CD) and 2 circles from batting.

3. Glue batting circles to both sides of the card stock / CD circle to make a "sandwich."

4. Carefully iron interfacing to the wrong side of both the embroidered strip and lining strip. To protect the embroidery, either press slowly with a low iron from the interfacing side or use a pressing cloth from the fabric side

5. Lay the lining piece on top of the embroidered strip, right sides together, so that the top edges butt up together. Sew a ¼″ (6mm) seam along the top edge. Fold out so that you have a large strip, and press toward the lining.

Fold this in half and match the side seams. Sew with a ¼″ (6mm) seam to make a tube. Press the seams open.

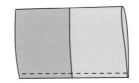

6. Fold the fabric bases into 4 quarters and press to obtain guide marks. Do the same with each end of your tube.

7. With right sides together, pin, matching the fold points, and sew the outer circular base to the outer fabric end of the tube. Pin and sew the lining base to the lining end of the tube, but leave an approximate 3½″ (9cm) gap open.

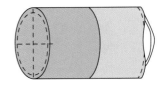

8. Turn the pot to the right side by pulling everything through the gap in the lining base.

9. Slip the CD sandwich into the gap in the lining base and either machine or hand sew the gap closed. Insert the lining inside the pot.

10. Working from the outside of pot, topstitch a line just under the lining "binding" to finish.

Tip You may find it easier to press the interfacing to the back of your embroidery before trimming, as it helps to stabilize the embroidery. If so, you will need a slightly bigger piece of interfacing.

This pretty brooch uses the veins of a leaf to create the stitch sections. Working with just one strand of Aurifil wool thread creates a fine delicate texture, with blanket stitch edging adding extra detail to finish. The easy handling of the felt makes for a very enjoyable, quick project … and I don't think you will be able to stop at just one! These make beautiful handmade gifts or could easily be adapted to become holiday ornaments.

Materials

GREEN WOOL FELT: 1 rectangle 4″ × 6″ (10 × 15cm)

PURPLE WOOL FELT: 1 rectangle 4″ × 6″ (10 × 15cm)

TRACING WHEEL

TRANSFER PEN/PENCIL

SAFETY PIN OR BROOCH CLIP

THREAD: 1 each of Aurifil 12-weight wool 54-yard (50m) spools in the following colors:

Outline: dark green (8897)

A: pale pink (8426)

B: mauve (8553)

C: apricot (8205)

D: variegated orange (8002)

E: orange (8215)

F: dusky pink (8401)

G: dull red (8442)

H: berry (8450)

stitches

1 Chain (page 19): 1 strand

2 Satin (page 19): 2 strands

3 Colonial knot (page 20): 1 strand

4 Seed (page 20): 1 strand

5 Running (page 20): 1 strand

7 Bullion knot: (page 21) 1 strand

15 Lazy daisy (bonus, page 40): 1 strand

18 Blanket (bonus, page 61): 1 strand

19 Buttonhole wheel (bonus, page 61): 1 strand

CONSTRUCTION

Preparation

From the green wool felt, using the Leaf Brooch pattern (page 104) and following the tracing instructions (see Tracing, page 13), mark the image onto the felt with the tracing wheel and marking pen. (*Note:* There is no need to use a hoop when working with felt.)

Stitching

1. Using backstitch and 1 strand of dark green (8897), stitch all the outlines. Stitch parallel straight stitches along the length of the center stem.

2. Following the stitch guide, fill each section with different stitches as shown.

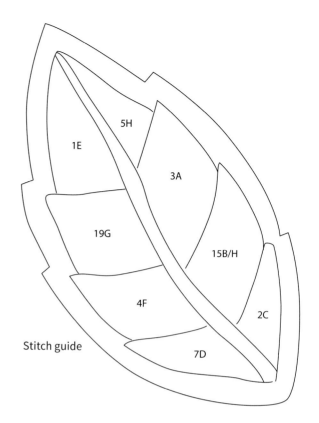

Stitch guide

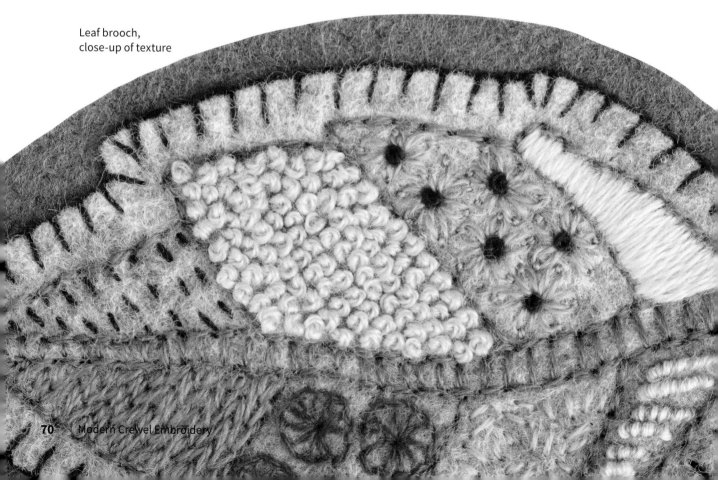

Leaf brooch,
close-up of texture

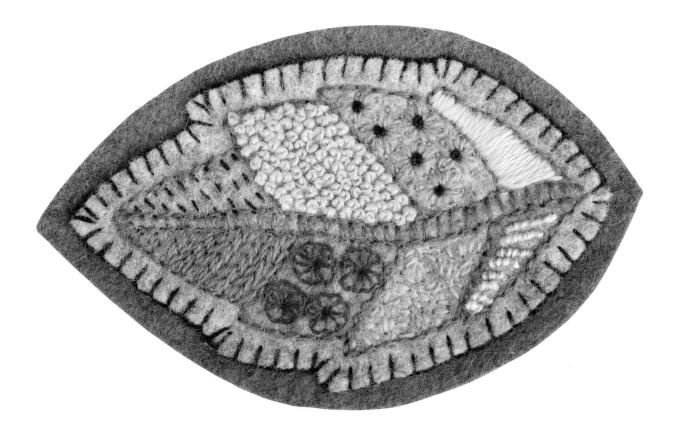

Making the Brooch

1. Carefully cut excess felt away from the embroidered leaf, leaving an approximate ³⁄₁₆″ (5mm) of felt around outline.

2. With both pieces right side up, pin to the purple felt square and sew together using blanket stitch and H berry (8450) around the outer edge.

3. Trim away excess felt, leaving an approximate ³⁄₁₆″ (5mm) of purple felt around the outline.

4. Using 2 strands of wool thread, stitch the safety pin to the back of the brooch.

Honeycomb Hoop

Finished project: 10″ × 10″ (25 × 25cm) • **Stitched area:** 7″ × 9″ (18 × 23cm)

Earlier projects in this book were inspired by free-motion quilting patterns. In this Geometrics section, the starting point often stems from one of the many patchwork patterns that are dear to my heart. We are going back to basics with the very first patchwork I ever did, age ten years old. Nowadays we call this **English paper piecing**, but back in the 1970s it was the only patchwork I knew. Hexagons are such a pleasing shape and filled with all those woolly textures, they started to remind me of honeycomb, so I just had to add a bee! This also led to the honey-toned color palette which, along with the brown background, makes the whole thing warm and comforting.

Materials

FABRIC: 13″ × 13″ (33 × 33cm) (I used Essex Linen Yard-Dyed "Leather," a cotton/linen blend by Robert Kaufman Fabrics.)

TRANSFER PEN/PENCIL

WOODEN HOOP: 10″ (25cm)

THREAD: 1 each of Aurifil 12-weight wool 54-yard (50m) spools in the following colors:

Outline hexagons: dark brown (8361)

Outline bee wings: pale gray (8600)

A: variegated yellow (8001)

B: pale yellow (8115)

C: yellow (8120)

D: dark yellow (8135)

E: pale orange (8205)

F: peach (8212)

G: orange (8235)

H: dark orange (8242)

I: variegated orange (8003)

J: black (8692)

K: gray (8082)

stitches

1 Chain (page 19): 2 strands

2 Satin (page 19): 2 strands

3 Colonial knot (page 20): 2 strands

4 Double-seed (page 20): 1 strand

5 Running (page 20): 1 strand

6 Split (page 21): 2 strands

8 Laid work (page 22): 2 strands

15 Lazy daisy (bonus, page 40): 1 strand

17 Woven rose (bonus, page 55): 2 strands

19 Buttonhole wheel (bonus, page 61): 1 strand

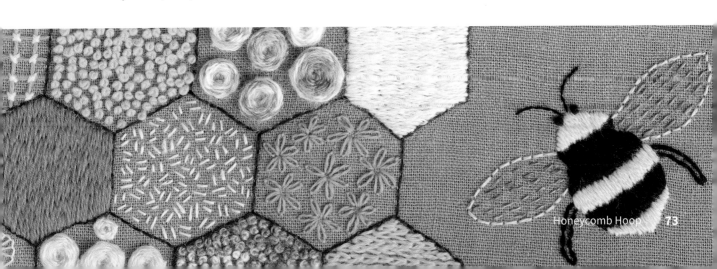

CONSTRUCTION

Preparation

Using the Honeycomb Hoop pattern (page 105) and following the tracing instructions (see Tracing, page 13), trace the image onto the fabric. Insert the fabric in the hoop (see Hooping, page 15).

Stitching

1. Using backstitch and 1 strand of dark brown (8361), stitch all the hexagon outlines.

2. Following the stitch guide, fill each hexagon with different stitches as shown.

3. To add variety, work your chain stitch and laid work in different directions each time they are used.

4. Work the body of the bee in satin stitch, using 2 strands of thread and alternating black and yellow stripes. The antennae are stitched using a single strand of black thread and backstitch. The legs are outlined with a double strand of black thread and backstitch. The eyes are double-stranded colonial knots in black.

5. For the wings, outline with a single strand of pale gray thread (8600) and a backstitch, filling with rows of running stitch in a single strand of gray thread.

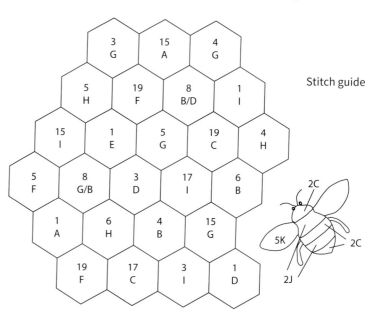

Stitch guide

Honeycomb hoop, close-up of texture

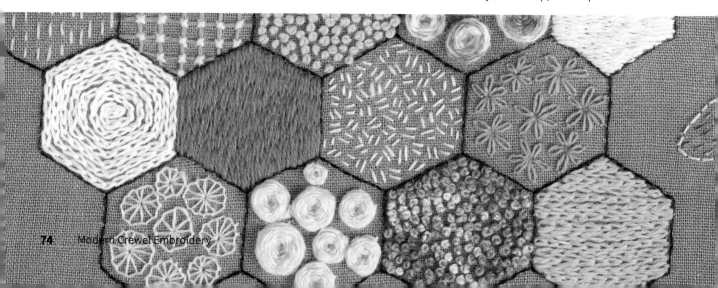

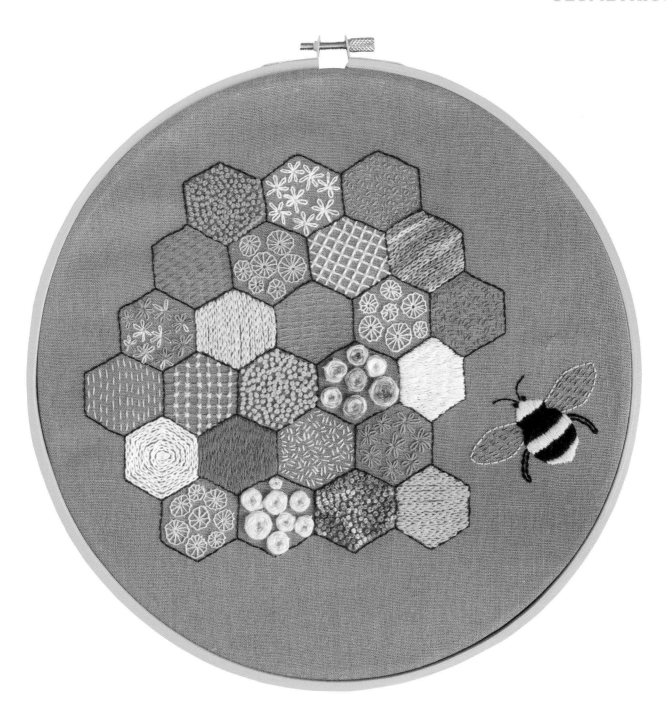

Finishing

If necessary, remove the fabric from the hoop to erase any tracing lines and re-insert in the hoop.

Follow the instructions to finish the hoop back (see Finishing a Hoop Back, page 16).

Patchwork Block Mini Hoops

Finished project: 4˝ × 4˝ (10 × 10cm) each • Stitched area: 3˝ × 3˝ (7.5 × 7.5cm)

In this section of the book, my two favorite crafts collide on more than one occasion. I have taken my inspiration from patchwork again for this trio of tiny geometric hoops, each based on a different quilt block. As before, three is the magic number, with different colorways making these mini hoops an extra-cute project. They would make lovely little gifts and could even be turned into Christmas tree decorations with a change of color palette. Or hang them in a row in your sewing room as a decoration.

Materials

FABRIC: 7″ × 21″ (18 × 53.5cm)
(I used Essex Linen Yarn-Dyed "Flax," a cotton/linen blend by Robert Kaufman Fabrics.)

TRANSFER PEN/PENCIL

WOODEN HOOPS (3): 4″ (10cm)

THREAD: 1 each of Aurifil 12-weight wool 54-yard (50m) spools in the following colors:

Outline: charcoal (8803)

For green hoop:

A: variegated green (8007)

B: dark green (8890)

C: green (8875)

D: pale green (8860)

For pink hoop:

A: mauve (8535)

B: magenta (8540)

C: pale mauve (8574)

D: variegated pink (8005)

For orange hoop:

A: raspberry red (8402)

B: red (8258)

C: variegated orange (8003)

D: peach (8212)

stitches

1 Chain (page 19): 2 strands

2 Satin (page 19): 2 strands

3 Colonial knot (page 20): 2 strands

4 Seed (page 20): 1 strand

5 Running (page 20): 1 strand

7 Bullion knot (page 21): 2 strands

8 Laid work (page 22): 2 strands

13 Spiderweb (bonus, page 31): 2 strands

CONSTRUCTION

Preparation

From the linen fabric, cut 3 squares 7″ × 7″ (18 × 18cm). Using the 3 Patchwork Block Mini Hoop (green / pink / orange) patterns (page 106) and following the tracing instructions (see Tracing, page 13), trace the image onto the fabric. Insert the fabric in the hoop (see Hooping, page 15).

Stitching

1. Using backstitch and 1 strand of charcoal (8803), stitch all the outlines.

2. Following the stitch guide, fill each section with different stitches as shown.

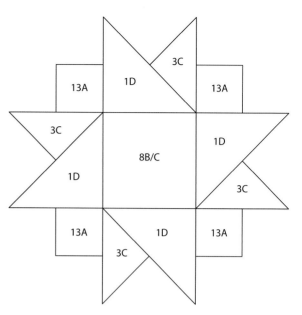

Green stitch guide

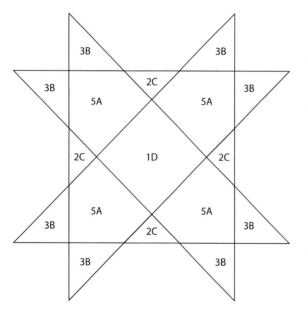

Pink stitch guide

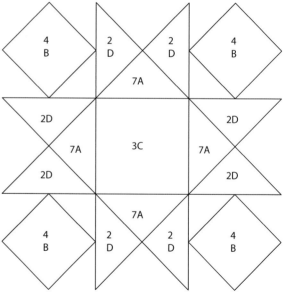

Orange stitch guide

Patchwork block mini hoops, close-up of texture

Finishing

If necessary, remove the fabric from the hoop to erase any tracing lines and re-insert it in the hoop.

Follow the instructions to finish the hoop back (see Finishing a Hoop Back, page 16).

Cosmic Belt

Finished project: 2″ × 42″ (5 × 106.5cm)
Stitched area: 1½″ × 39½″ (4 × 100cm)

A fabric belt seemed the perfect clothing item to decorate with crewelwork, and this simple circles-within-circle motif will add some pizzaz to any outfit. I've used Appletons crewel wool here in a zingy palette of colors. The middle circles are worked in different stitches with a blanket stitch edging used for each outer ring. This is an unusual shape of fabric to embroider and you will need to move your hoop along the strip, stitching two circles at a time.

I asked my son, who has his own blacksmithing forge, to make the buckle for me, which has made this item extra special. If you're not lucky enough to have a blacksmith in the family, then you will find plenty of choices online—or why not check your closet for an old belt with a nice buckle, or look for one at your local thrift store? The denim look of the linen means it should go with all sorts of outfits. I plan to wear mine with a big white New Romantic style shirt and a velvet waistcoat.

Materials

FABRIC: 12″ × 46″ (30.5 × 117cm)
(I used Essex Linen Yarn-Dyed "Cadet," a cotton/linen blend by Robert Kaufman Fabrics.)

TRANSFER PEN/PENCIL

WOODEN HOOP: 6″ (15cm)

BELT BUCKLE

TAILORS AWL

IRON-ON INTERFACING: 4″ × 42½″ (5 × 108cm)

THREAD: 1 each of Appletons Crewel Wool 25m (27.3 yards) skeins in the following colors:

Outline: black (998)

A: orange (441)

B: pale orange (862)

C: red (502)

D: yellow (844)

E: green (434)

F: pale green (423)

G: pale turquoise (483)

H: turquoise (485)

I: purple (454)

J: magenta (003)

K: pink (801)

stitches

1	Chain (page 19): 1 strand
3	Colonial knot (page 20): 1 strand
4	Seed (page 20): 1 strand
5	Running (page 20): 1 strand
7	Bullion knot (page 21): 1 strand
8	Laid work (page 22): 1 strand
13	Spiderweb (bonus, page 31): 2 strands
18	Blanket (bonus, page 61): 1 strand

CONSTRUCTION

Preparation

From the linen fabric, cut a strip 4″ × 46″ (10 × 117cm) and put aside. Using the Cosmic Belt pattern (page 107) and following the tracing instructions (see Tracing, page 13), trace the image onto the remaining fabric. You will need to move along the length of fabric, tracing 3 circles at a time and matching the outer lines. Insert the first stitching area in the hoop (see Hooping, page 15).

Stitching

1. Sew around each outer ring using a blanket stitch in the color indicated in the stitch guide for each circle.

2. Fill the inner circles with different stitches as shown in the stitch guide.

3. Sew a line of running stitches in black (998) around each outer circle close to the edge.

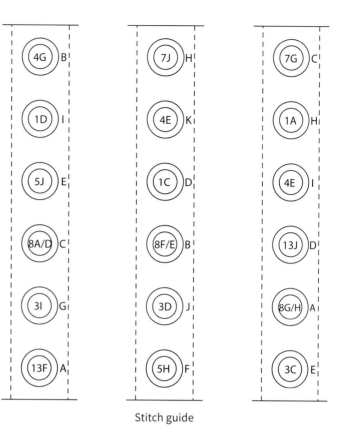

Stitch guide

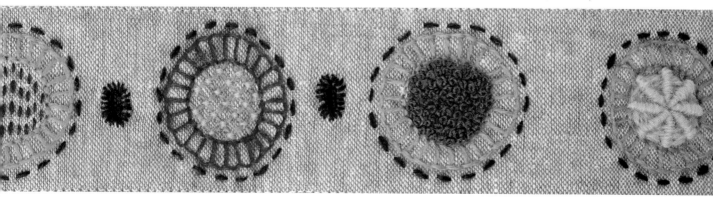

Cosmic belt, close-up of texture

Making the Belt

1. Remove the fabric from hoop to erase any tracing lines and press carefully. Trim to a 2½″ × 43″ (6.5 × 109cm) strip.

2. From the 4″ (10cm) strip of fabric, cut 1 strip 1⅜″ × 4¾″ (3.5 × 12cm) for the belt loop and 1 strip 2½″ × 43″ (6.5 × 109cm) for the belt back.

3. From iron-on interfacing, cut 2 strips 2″ × 42½″ (5 × 108cm) and press to the back of the embroidered strip and belt back, centering so that ¼″ (6mm) is clear all the way around.

4. Place the belt strips right sides together and stitch along one long edge. Press ¼″ (6mm) seam allowance to the wrong side on the belt along all 3 free sides. Pin the wrong sides together and topstitch neatly close to the edge around all 4 sides of the belt.

5. Fold ¼″ (6mm) seam allowance over on both long sides of the belt loop. Fold in half, pin, and topstitch along both long sides.

6. Using a tailor's awl, make a hole in the belt through both layers 1¼″ (3cm) away from the edge at the end where the buckle will sit. Use small, sharp scissors to enlarge the hole so it is big enough for the belt prong. With black thread (998), sew blanket stitches very close together around the edge of the hole to neaten.

7. Place the belt loop around the belt and pin the raw ends so that they meet at the back of the belt, close to the buckle end. Thread the belt end through the buckle with the prong through the hole, and pin the end of the belt over, covering the raw edges of the loop. Hand stitch the belt end in place at the back of the belt, using a strong thread and stitching through the belt loop at the same time.

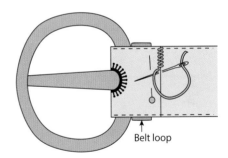

Belt loop

8. Using the tailor's awl and the small, sharp scissors, carefully make a series of small holes, just big enough for the prong, between the embroidered circles at the other end of the belt and where needed. Sew a blanket stitch around each as before.

Depending on the size required, you may need to make the belt longer or add an extra belt loop.

Mandala Hoop

Finished project: 10″ × 10″ (25.5 × 25.5cm)
Stitched area: 8½″ × 8½″ (21.5 × 21.5cm)

As I said in the introduction, I find embroidery very meditative and mindful, and so this was an obvious choice for a design subject. A mandala is a geometric design that represents wholeness and the universe. Through contemplation to the point of saturation, a mandala is thought to help you gain a meditative state of mind. If this is correct, then with all the hours you will spend stitching this design, you should be very calm and relaxed by the end of it!

This design stands out from the others as it uses heavy, dense stitches rather than decorative ones, and the choice of both stitches and colors is more restricted. To stop the stitched areas appearing too saturated, I used the outlining charcoal thread to create decorative bands that break up the blocks of color. This also means I can introduce you to the most straightforward stitch in the book as this project's bonus stitch. I have chosen bright, jewel-like thread colors and another of the hand-dyed Osnaburg cottons in a warm sunset shade. These elements go together to evoke a new age hippie vibe full of peace and love. Hang this on your wall and gaze it at when you need to de-stress.

Materials

FABRIC: 13″ × 13″ (33 × 33cm)
(I used Hand-Dyed Osnaburg in "Day Lily,"
a cotton fabric with a linen-like texture by
Fiber on a Whim.)

TRANSFER PEN/PENCIL

BRIGHT PINK FELT: 10 × 10″ (25.5 × 25.5cm)

WOODEN HOOP: 10″ (25cm)

THREAD: 1 each of Aurifil 12-weight wool
54-yard (50m) spools in the following colors:

Outline: charcoal (8083)

A: pale turquoise (8823)

B: turquoise (8810)

C: orange (8235)

D: magenta (8540)

E: hot pink (8530)

stitches

1 Chain (page 19): 2 strands

2 Satin (page 19): 2 strands

3 Colonial knot (page 20): 2 strands

6 Split (page 21): 2 strands

11 Felt appliqué (page 23)

13 Spiderweb (bonus, page 31): 2 strands

20 Straight (bonus, page 87): 1 strand

Mandala Hoop

CONSTRUCTION

Preparation

Using the Mandala Hoop design pattern (page 107) and following the tracing instructions (see Tracing, page 13), trace the image onto the fabric. Insert the fabric in the hoop (see Hooping, page 15).

Stitching

1. Using backstitch and 1 strand of charcoal (8083), stitch all the outlines except those around the felt appliqué (#11) outer dome shapes. Use 1 strand of the same thread to stitch straight stitches to create decorative rings and arches as indicated in the guide. Use 2 strands of the same thread to fill the adjacent ring with equally spaced colonial knots, along with alternate borders on the outer arches.

Stitch guide

2. Following the stitch guide, fill each section with different stitches as shown.

3. Using the Mandala Hoop appliqué pattern (page 108), cut out 8 felt pieces. Pin them in place over each #11 shape as indicated in the stitch guide and stitch down with matching thread (see Felt Appliqué, page 23). Using 1 strand of charcoal (8083), stitch the outlines around the felt.

Mandala hoop, close-up of texture

20 *Straight Stitch*

This is such a simple motion that it doesn't even require a diagram. It is simply one straight stitch, with the needle coming out at one point and going in again a stitch length away. In this project, we are using the straight stitches to add decorative rings and arches, and the width of the stitch is determined by the shape. Try to keep your stitches equal distance apart. I found it helpful to use the backstitches on the ring outline as a placement guide. Your stitches will need to slant slightly as they curve, especially around the tighter arches.

Finishing

If necessary, remove the fabric from the hoop to erase any tracing lines and re-insert it in the hoop. Follow the instructions to finish the hoop back (see Finishing a Hoop Back, page 16).

Clamshell Pillow

Finished project: 12″ × 12″ (30.5 × 30.5cm)
Stitched area: 10″ × 10″ (25.5 × 25.5cm)

Our last design is a big one, and it includes almost all the stitches we've been practicing so far. It was inspired by yet another favorite patchwork pattern and one that works particularly well as a pillow. I decided to create an ombré effect by stitching each row in a different shade, which washes down through the colors in a gentle ripple. I love this colorwash effect and have made similar ombré clamshell pillows using fabric. Using the same stitch and color for each clamshell in a row creates a new twist on the sampler genre and one that works well for interior decor. This would make a special small pillow to adorn a bed or a statement chair, one suited more to decoration rather than heavy usage.

Materials

FABRIC: 15″ × 35″ (38 × 90cm)
(I used Essex Linen Yarn-Dyed "Bleached White," a cotton/linen blend by Robert Kaufman Fabrics.)

TRANSFER PEN/PENCIL

WOODEN HOOP: 10″ (25cm)

PILLOW FORM: 12″ (30.5cm)

THREAD: 1 each of Aurifil 12-weight wool 54-yard (50m) spools in the following colors:

Outline: brown (8320)

A: mauve (8553)

B: pale pink (8426)

C: dusky pink (8431)

D: orange (8215)

E: peach (8212)

F: yellow (8130)

G: lemon (8112)

H: mint (8898)

I: pale turquoise (8865)

J: turquoise (8850)

K: petrol blue (8820)

stitches

1 Chain (page 19): 2 strands

3 Colonial knot (page 20): 2 strands

4 Double-seed (page 20): 1 strand

5 Running (page 20): 1 strand

8 Laid work (page 22): 2 strands

10 Star (page 22): 1 strand

13 Spiderweb (bonus, page 31): 2 strands

15 Lazy daisy (bonus, page 40): 1 strand

16 Fly (bonus, page 51): 2 strands

17 Woven rose (bonus, page 55): 2 strands

19 Buttonhole wheel (bonus, page 61): 1 strand

CONSTRUCTION

Preparation

From the Essex linen fabric, cut a square 15″ × 15″ (38 × 38cm). Using the Clamshell Pillow (page 108) and following the tracing instructions (see Tracing, page 13), trace the image onto the fabric. Insert the fabric in the hoop (see Hooping, page 15).

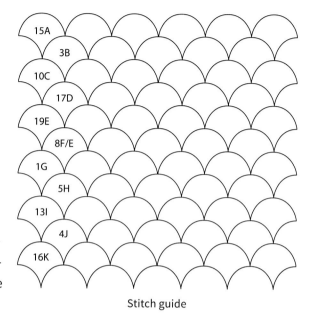

Stitch guide

Stitching

1. Using backstitch and 1 strand of brown (8320), stitch all the outlines.

2. Following the stitch guide, fill each row of clamshells with different stitches as shown. Each clamshell in a row is filled by the same stitch and shade as indicated in the first clamshell on the guide.

Make the Pillow

1. Remove from the hoop to erase any tracing lines and press carefully. Trim to a 13″ × 13″ (33 × 33cm) square.

2. From the remainder of the linen fabric, cut 2 rectangles 10″ × 13″ (25.5 × 33cm). Turn over a ½″ (1cm) hem twice on a 13″ (33cm) side on one of the pieces. Pin and then stitch along to hem. Repeat with the other backing piece. Press.

3. Lay the embroidered front, right side up. Lay the 2 back pieces on top, right sides down, overlapping the seamed edges in the center. Pin all the way around and stitch, using a ½″ (1cm) seam allowance. Snip the corners, turn right side out, and press. Insert a pillow form.

Clamshells embroidery, close-up of texture

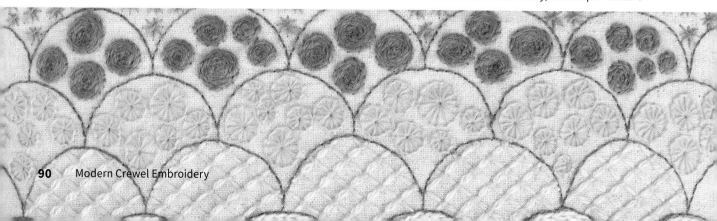

PATTERNS

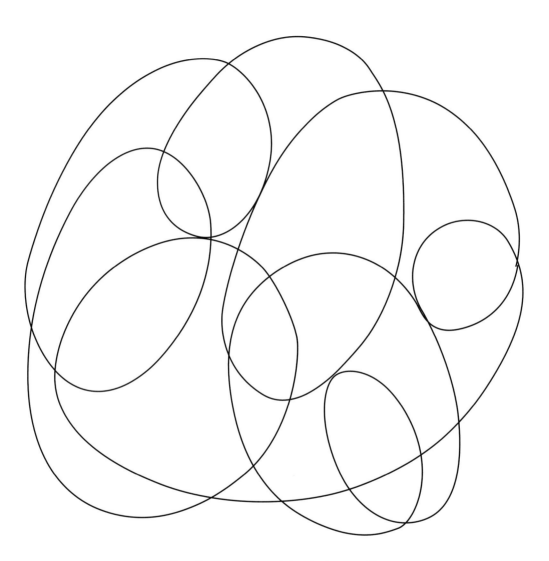

Doodle Hoop (page 24)—design motif

Labyrinth Pouch (page 28)—
design motif

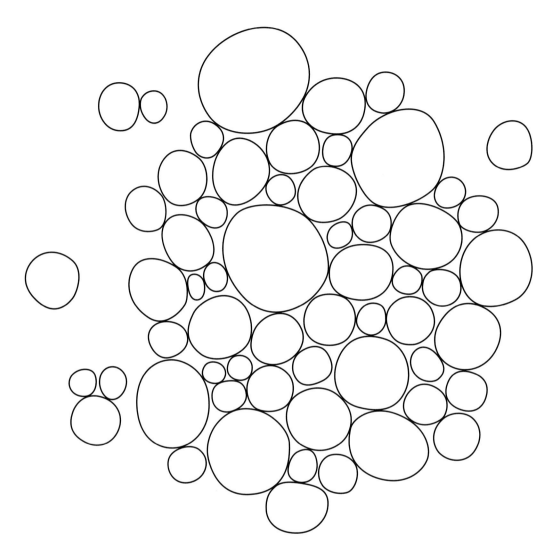

Bubbles Hoop (page 34)—design motif

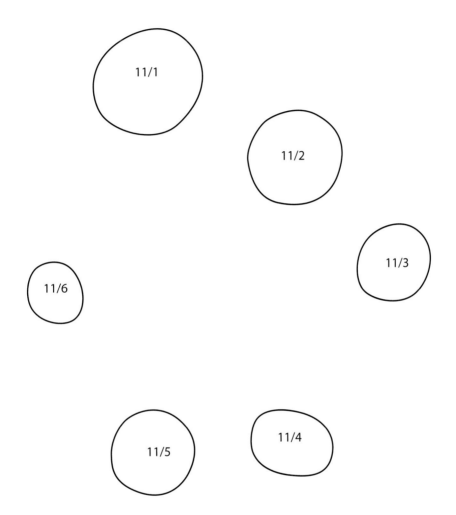

Bubbles Hoop (page 34)—bubbles/circle appliqués

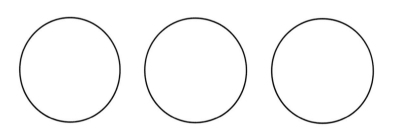

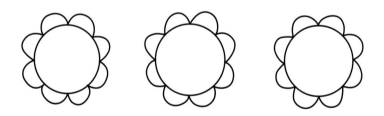

Shapes Pincushion Trio (page 38)—design shapes

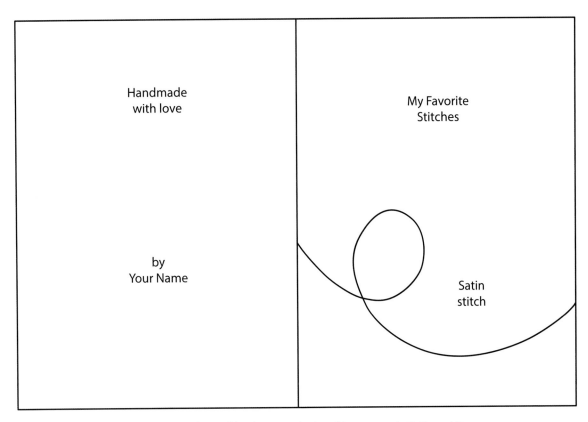

Handmade
with love

by
Your Name

My Favorite
Stitches

Satin
stitch

Loops Stitch Booklet (page 42)—booklet pages 1, 2, 7, and 8

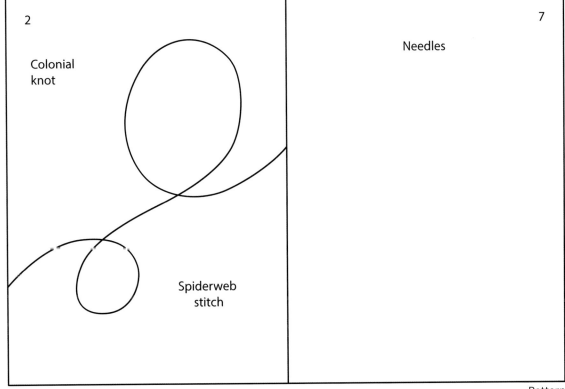

2

7

Colonial
knot

Needles

Spiderweb
stitch

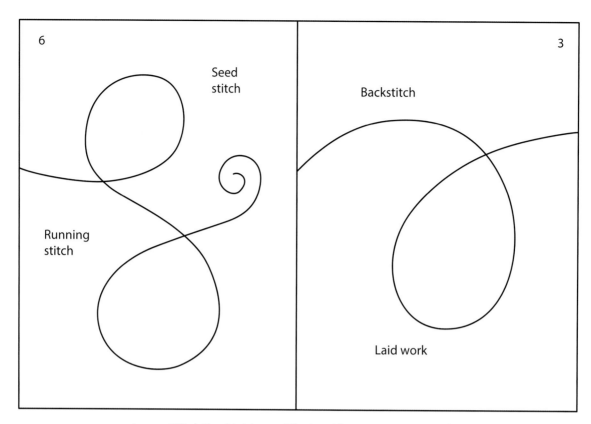

Loops Stitch Booklet (page 42)—booklet pages 3, 4, 5, and 6

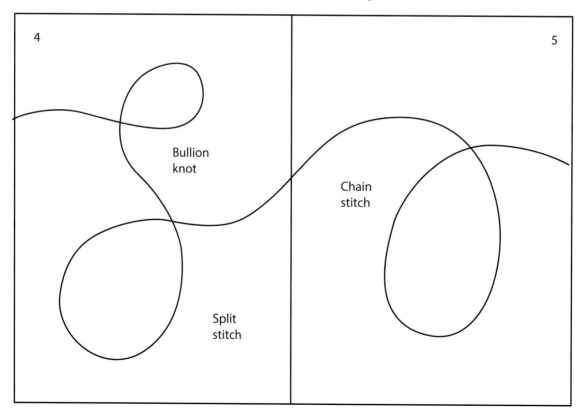

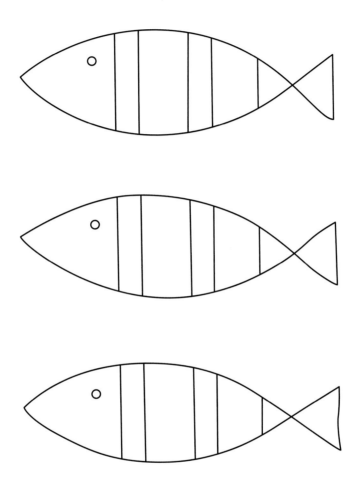

Scandi Fish Hoop (page 48)

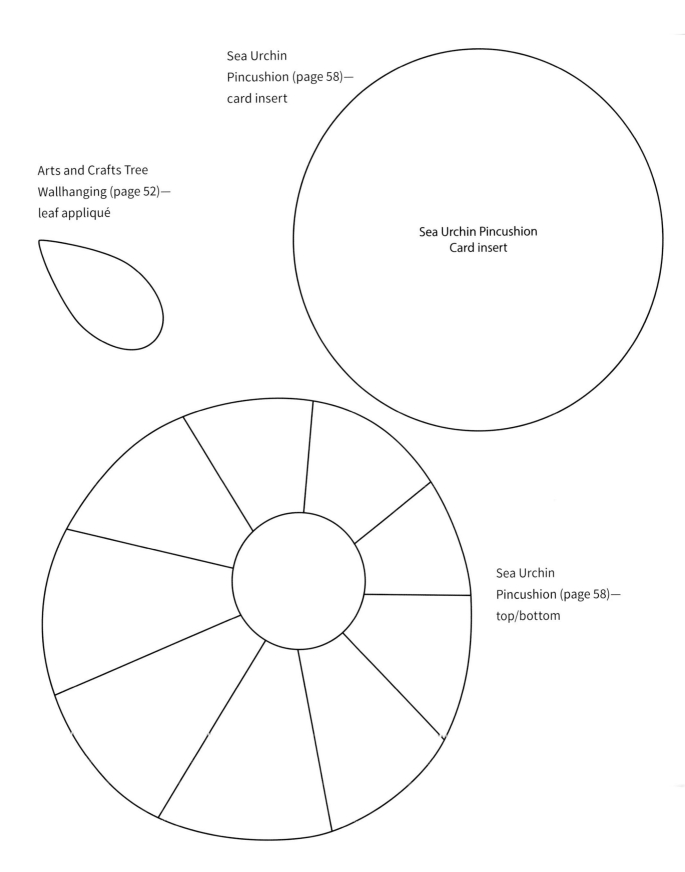

Sea Urchin
Pincushion (page 58)—
card insert

Arts and Crafts Tree
Wallhanging (page 52)—
leaf appliqué

Sea Urchin Pincushion
Card insert

Sea Urchin
Pincushion (page 58)—
top/bottom

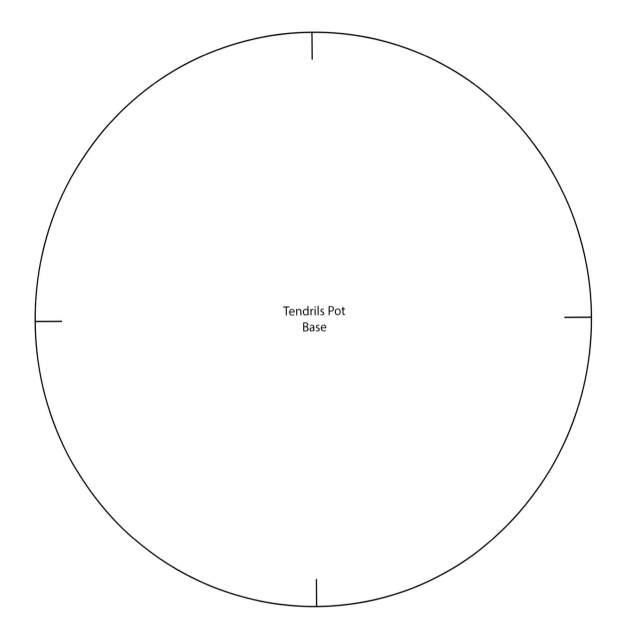

Tendrils Pot
Base

Tendrils Pot (page 64)—base

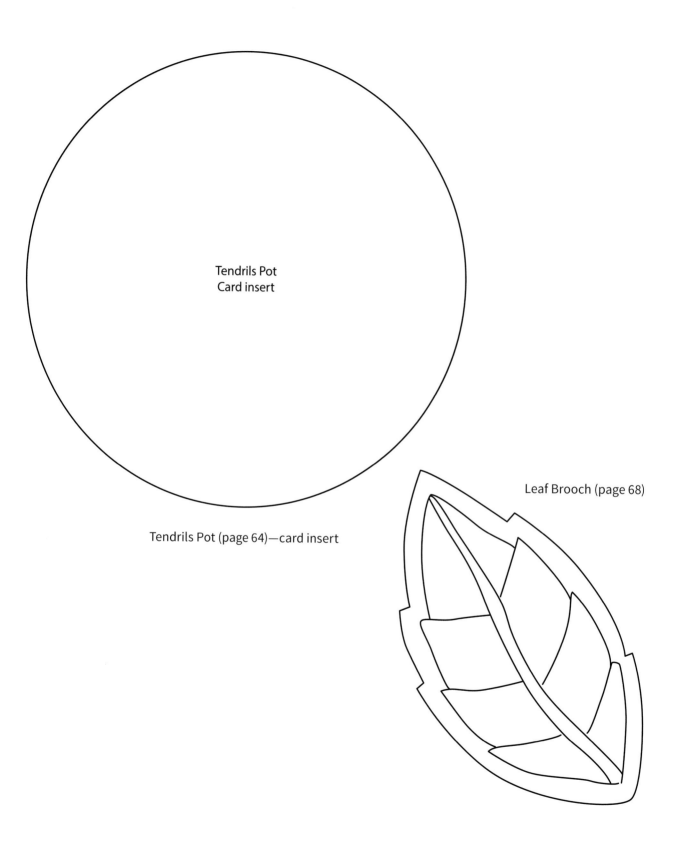

Tendrils Pot
Card insert

Tendrils Pot (page 64)—card insert

Leaf Brooch (page 68)

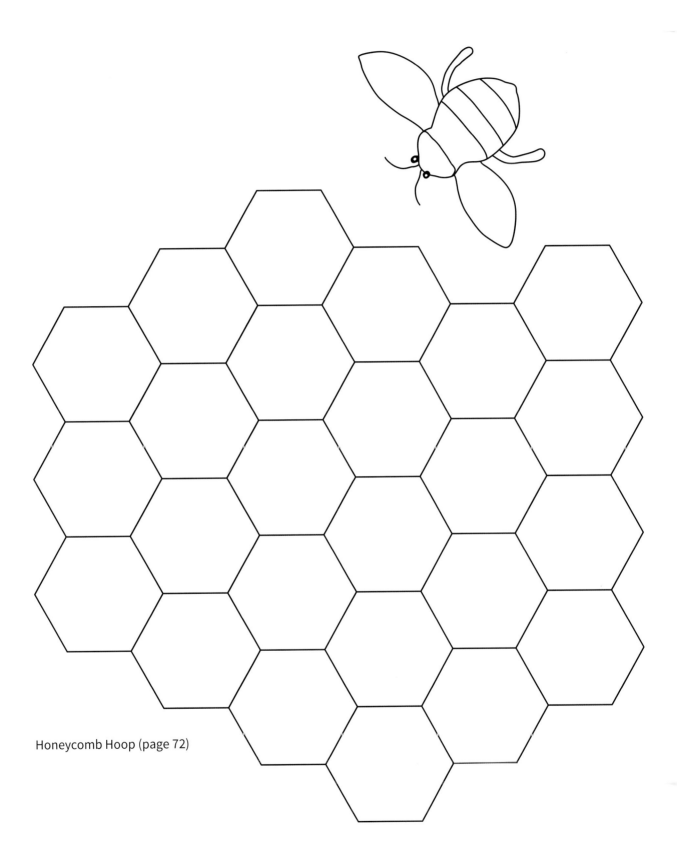

Honeycomb Hoop (page 72)

Patchwork Block Mini Hoop (page 76)—
green hoop design

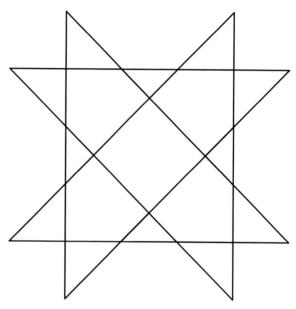

Patchwork Block Mini Hoop (page 76)—
pink hoop design

Patchwork Block Mini Hoop (page 76)—
orange hoop design

Mandala Hoop (page 84)—design motif

Cosmic Belt (page 80)

Mandala Hoop (page 84)—
mandala appliqué

Clamshell Pillow (page 88)

RESOURCES

THREADS AND FABRICS

Aurifil   aurifil.com

• My Aurifil 12-weight wool collections Modern Crewelwork and Stitching with Wool—*the latter accompanies this book and contains many of the wool threads used here*—are available from my website (for UK, stitchgathering.co.uk) and from Morris Textiles (for USA, morristextiles.com).

• I have produced a downloadable chart to convert Aurifil wool thread to DMC, which you can find on my website: stitchgathering.co.uk > *click* Aurifil Wool Conversion Chart

Appletons   appletons.org.uk
Crewel wool

Fiber on a Whim   fiberonawhim.com
Hand-dyed Osnaburg cotton

Linladan   linladan.com
Vintage Swedish threads

Robert Kaufman Fabrics   robertkaufman.com
Essex Linen and Manchester Linen

Zweigart   zweigart.de/?lang=en
Superior embroidery linens

HOOPS

Auburn Hoops   auburnhoops.co
Unusual and beautiful wooden hoops

Elbesee   elbesee.co.uk
My favorite hoops for stitching

EXTRA

The Great Tapestry of Scotland
scotlandstapestry.com

• View the tapestry at the Visitors Center at Galashiels in the Scottish Borders. For more information on this amazing piece of community art, I recommend the book *The Great Tapestry of Scotland* by Alistair Moffat (Birlinn Ltd.; ISBN 9781780271606).

ABOUT THE AUTHOR

Jo Avery lives in the countryside near Edinburgh in Scotland surrounded by woodland and wildlife. She began her career in textiles and entrepreneurship at age 21 with her first business, Cleopatra's Needle, which designed and produced needlepoint kits. She learned to make quilts soon after and continued to pursue this as a hobby while bringing up a family and partnering her husband, Jonathan Avery in their furniture and retail business.

A decade ago, she discovered quilting blogs and began her own, *myBearpaw*. A whole new career sprang from this: teaching crafts and designing quilt and embroidery patterns.

She now teaches far and wide, designs quilts and embroideries for a number of magazines, and organizes quilt retreats, both physical and virtual. She is one-third of The Thread House collective and is a certified Aurifilosopher. Her first solo book, *New Patchwork & Quilting Basics*, was published by Stash Books.

Photo by Jonathan Avery

Visit Jo online and follow on social media!

Website: stitchgathering.co.uk

Blog: joavery.co.uk

Instagram: @joaverystitch

ALSO BY JO AVERY: